Field Guide to
COCKTAILS

How to Identify and Prepare Virtually Every Mixed Drink at the Bar

By Rob Chirico

QUIRK BOOKS
PHILADELPHIA

DISCLAIMER

This volume attempts to be as comprehensive as possible, but new cocktails seem to be created every minute, and one could fill a worthy tome with just the names of the new Martinis being concocted alone. The major entries in this guide are a jumping-off point for understanding the fundamentals of mixing each recipe, and the accompanying variations are examples and samples of each cocktail's possibilities.

Library of Congress Cataloging in Publication Number: 2005921505

ISBN: 1-59474-063-1

Printed in Singapore

Typeset in Adobe Garamond, Franklin Gothic, and Impact

Designed by Karen Onorato
Edited by Erin Slonaker
Photography by Steve Legato
Iconography by Karen Onorato

Distributed in North America by Chronicle Books
85 Second Street
San Francisco, CA 94105

10 9 8 7 6 5 4 3 2 1

Quirk Books
215 Church Street
Philadelphia, PA 19106
www.quirkbooks.com

Contents

Introduction

It was not so long ago that the search for a classic cocktail glass, the ubiquitous Martini glass, would often turn up dry. In 1973 in *Esquire*, James Villas proclaimed, "Young people do not like martinis, and they're not drinking them. Ever! Anywhere!" The Martini, however, is alive and flourishing—as are countless other cocktails. From old favorites like the Old Fashioned that were sipped by our grandparents to new trendsetters like the Cosmopolitan, cocktails are joyously being discovered and rediscovered everywhere. Selecting the right cocktail from the array of potables being shaken and stirred can be overwhelming. The purpose of this easy-to-carry guide is to familiarize the reader with classic cocktails, their contemporary progeny, and some drinks that were once the rage but are now all but forgotten. As a practical reference, it is designed for the reader eager to know what to look for in an authentic Daiquiri as well as for the aspiring home bartender who wants to master muddling and mixing a Brazilian Caipirinha.

Each entry includes recipes, some historical or anecdotal background, and purchasing information. You'll learn what rye whiskey is and why it should be used in a Manhattan, how to layer drinks, where not to order a Margarita, and how to modify your cocktails to suit your taste and that of your guests. Every recipe also includes a helpful section on food pairings—an area almost patently neglected in most cocktail books.

In this age of automated supermarket checkouts, cash machines, and self-serve gasoline pumps, the cocktail, too, is often in jeopardy of being mass-produced and premixed, but armed with this guide you can keep the art of mixology alive. Among the many stalwart bartenders who are proponents of true mixology, New York barmen Dale DeGroff and Gary Regan are the leaders in their field, and readers will come upon their names throughout this book.

Before we begin, let us briefly explore what a cocktail is and where it comes from. This would be a simple matter if we knew its origin—but we don't. Naturally, speculation abounds. The word *cocktail* has been linked to a seventeenth-century British concoction of chicken broth and ale called "cock ale"; to the French *coquetel*, from *coquetier*, for the "egg cups" in which Antoine Peychaud served brandy and bitters (see **Sazerac**); and to the dregs at the bottom of barrels called "cock-tailings." Although its origin is elusive, the word *cocktail* was in general use by the early 1800s. In its unadorned state, the cocktail is a mixture of two or more ingredients. Embellished, the cocktail is the soul of conviviality and a prelude to adventure. The situations and times to order or mix cocktails are endless, but there is probably nothing more therapeutic than sitting down with friends or a loved one after an arduous day for the venerable cocktail hour.

Behind Bars—An Insider's Look at Ordering Out

The recipes in this guide—and practically all cocktail books—have been formulated to make a small number of drinks at a time. Most bars and bartenders do not have the luxury of precisely measuring out drinks. With one eye on their time and the other trained on management's expenses, bartenders generally standardize amounts out of necessity as well as for consistency. In fact, most standard mixed drinks contain 3 ounces of liquid; a Martini, for example, will have 3 ounces of straight alcohol, while a gin and tonic on the rocks will have 1 ounce gin and 2 ounces tonic. A bar shot glass, however big or heavy, typically contains just 1 ounce, and many bars require measured 1-ounce drink pourers on bottles. Think of that next time you order three shots of Stoli when you could have ordered a "bone-dry" (i.e., no vermouth) Stoli Martini at less than half the price. I have seen savvy customers order bone-dry Jägermeister Martinis to the same end. Here are a few other tips from behind the bar:

• Spirits fall into three categories: well or rail (generic), call (name brand), and top-shelf (costly name brand). Know what you want and be specific when you order—otherwise, you will be given well, which is usually not very good.

• Don't assume. If you want a Gin Martini, ask for one—and, again, preferably by brand. Don't be surprised if, when you ask for a Martini, you receive a Vodka Martini on the rocks with a twist instead of the anticipated straight-up Gin Martini with olives. The same goes for Alexanders, Stingers, and any number of other drinks.

• Many bars will "supersize" drinks like a Margarita for an additional fee, but be aware that usually little or no alcohol is added to the extra ice and mix.

• Don't be afraid to try a new drink the bartender recommends. It often leads to an earlier "buyback," or a drink on the house.

• Bartenders are responsible for your safety and the safety of others. They have every right not to serve you if they think you are "in the red"—that you have had too much to drink—and they are required to call the police if you leave and choose to drive while intoxicated.

• If you really want to alienate your bartender, try clapping your hands or snapping your fingers to get attention.

• Bartenders are not out to cheat you; they depend on your tips. If you think the drinks are too small, the management is probably responsible. Don't take it out on the bartender.

A Note on the Headings

The drinks presented here are primary cocktails, and most include cocktails with similar ingredients or themes. The mere fact that you can replicate any recipe precludes extinction; however, there are drinks on the "endangered species" list—drinks that have had their heyday but are now rarely, if ever, served. These are denoted by the following icon: ⚠. Each entry is accompanied by a heading that provides a general description of the cocktail, including what is known of its history, the origin of its name, and its creator. "Purchase" refers to the best places to buy these cocktails as well as when they should be practiced by the home bartender. The ideal times and places to sip your cocktails are discussed under "Areas and Time of Occurrence," and the appropriate months of the year to have them are briefly noted in "Season." "Preparation" enumerates ways to make the cocktail, along with methods of serving and any pertinent information particular to that cocktail.

A unique feature of this book is the category "Flavor Affinities." We are accustomed to breaking down food into four essential flavors: salty, sweet, sour, and bitter. Cocktails, too, are blends of distinct flavors. Is there anyone who drinks straight gin or vermouth at room temperature? But mix them together over ice in the right proportions, add a garnish, and you have a gift from the gods. You choose an olive or a twist of lemon peel for a dry Martini, but notice how you will never add a maraschino cherry. Since cocktails are complex mixtures to begin with, food pairings must be chosen carefully. The wrong food will destroy the identity of a cocktail, and the food in turn will be diminished.

It is not long after the cocktail is poured and the first sip savored that the happy recipient begins the search for something to nibble on. Cocktails cry out for food, and we often settle for a bowl of nuts or pretzels. But victuals are every bit as important as the beverage. Although a recent trend among creative bartenders has been to pair main dishes with cocktails, the cocktails are rarely served with dinner itself. Drinking a Martini while eating pasta with Bolognese sauce would do a cruel injustice to both. Food and drink must contrast and complement. Sweeter drinks are more accommodating to a variety of flavors and pair well with salty, fruity, and spicy dishes. A sip of a sweet Mai Tai welcomes the crunch of a crisp scallion pancake with a pungent ginger dipping sauce, but just as you would not consider a cherry for a Martini, avoid anything sweet or syrupy with drier cocktails. The temperature of your food, too, is as essential as that of your drink. Lukewarm dim sum are no better than a room-temperature Margarita; a shrimp cocktail that has lost its chill is as much a crime as cold Hot Buttered Rum.

In the pages that follow, I have attempted to present as many different food pairings as possible. The foods listed with a Daiquiri would go equally well with a Mojito, and the accompaniments for a Brandy Alexander would pair perfectly with a Black Russian. Once you recognize the basis for the makeup of your cocktail, rely on your intuition to guide you and use your imagination to inspire you. On a slightly scientific note, the liver metabolizes about one drink per hour; any more than this will build up in the bloodstream, causing the imbiber to suffer ill effects even after he or she has stopped drinking. Nothing can alter the time needed to metabolize alcohol, but you can slow down its absorption by pairing your drinks with fatty, high-protein foods like buffalo wings or burgers.

Equipment: The Right Tools for the Job

New cocktail recipes appear to increase exponentially each day, and so do the numerous gadgets and trappings for mixing, muddling, and measuring. With few exceptions, however, these useful contraptions and eye-pleasing paraphernalia are all variations on the tools listed below. The following is an extensive list for a well-equipped home bar. Essentials for a start-up bar are marked with an asterisk (*).

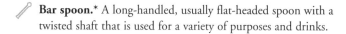

Bar spoon.* A long-handled, usually flat-headed spoon with a twisted shaft that is used for a variety of purposes and drinks.

Bar towels.* You should have at least one large, thin cotton towel just for drying glasses, and a few other dish towels for cleaning up spills.

Bottle and can openers.* In an age of pop-tops and screw caps, some people may never have encountered either of these types of openers, but the finer beers will require a bottle opener and larger juice cans will need can openers.

Channel knife. This is a flat piece of steel with a small, sharp opening through which you can cut long spirals of lemon peel.

Chef's knife. Use this for large fruits.

Citrus juicer* (with a bowl, a reamer, and holes to catch seeds and pulp) or a **citrus reamer**.

Coasters and bar napkins. Most kitchenware and gadget sections of stores have inexpensive festive coasters and napkins for all occasions. Keep a lively assortment on hand.

Cocktail shaker.* Shakers are readily available in various shapes, sizes, and materials, but a good cocktail shaker is always made of heavy stainless steel. This guarantees the coldest of drinks. If you can find an antique sterling silver shaker, all the better, but the common "silver bullet" shaker of stainless steel will serve you well. Most bars use what is called a Boston shaker. The bottom half of this shaker is stainless steel, and the top is glass. This versatile tool doubles as a tall mixing glass for stirred drinks.

Coil-rimmed cocktail strainer (Hawthorne strainer).* This familiar bar tool that fits over a metal shaker is sold everywhere, but you should look for one that is sturdy and will not uncoil like a stray bedspring.

Cork stopper with a no-drip pouring end. Drink pourers are mostly uniform, but cork stoppers will fit most any bottle. They are also excellent for leftover wine.

Corkscrews.* The common, pocket-size waiter's corkscrew with a folding knife to cut the foil of a wine bottle is perhaps the most common. If you prefer a wing-type corkscrew, look for one with an open curly screw rather than those that look more like a drill bit. The rabbit type of lever pullers are also excellent, but be warned that cheap ones may resemble their frightfully expensive cousins, but they won't last nearly as long.

Cutting boards.* Although a bar environment presents less chance of contamination than a kitchen, pure wood is losing favor to polyethylene (plastic) and composite wooden boards because the latter are less likely to harbor germs.

Electric all-purpose juicer for heavy-duty juicing. If you enjoy fruit drinks, the models available today are quick and have settings to select the amount of pulp desired.

Electric blender.* Choose a high-speed blender with a heavy-duty motor.

Large and small funnels.* Smaller funnels are perfect for daily use, but a time will come when you need to pour large quantities at a time, and a small funnel simply will not do.

Glass dishes for olives, limes, and other garnishes.* Like napkins and coasters, many attractive dishes are available in kitchenware stores.

Glass pitcher.* You will need a pitcher for all your stirred cocktails. Be sure that it is large enough to accommodate enough ice to get your drinks properly chilled.

Ice crusher. Electric ice crushers are expensive, but worth it if you entertain frequently. The small mallet-type variety is fine for most occasions.

Ice pick. The familiar, single-point ice pick was designed for large blocks, which you rarely see anymore. Newer picks for breaking up smaller quantities tend to look like heavy-duty forks.

Ice tongs and a bucket.* Glass may look nice here, but you will need a large, insulated bucket to prevent your ice from swimming away.

Jiggers and shot glasses.* Whether measured glasses or stainless-steel, double-sided cups, these come in various sizes: usually 1/2 ounce, 1 ounce, 2 ounces, and 1 1/2 ounces.

Julep strainer.* Use this mini colander with mixing glasses.

Measuring spoons and cups.* These are exactly the same as you probably have for your kitchen, but get a set of each solely for the bar.

Mixing glass.* (See "Cocktail shaker," above.)

Muddler. A wooden rod rather like a pestle used for crushing or "muddling" fruit.

Nutmeg grater. Since preground nutmeg pales by comparison to freshly grated whole nutmeg, this grater is vital for drinks that call for this spice.

Paring knife.* A thin, 4-inch, spear-tipped blade is essential for any bar. The edge must be kept as sharp as possible.

Pourers. Bars have drink pourers on their bottles for speedy pouring. Since the turnover of spirits in a home bar is more limited, buy pourers with caps to prevent the alcohol from evaporating.

Straws, swizzle sticks, and toothpicks.* Once again, kitchenware stores abound in these bar essentials.

Two-pronged olive or cherry grabber. A fork will do, but these handy utensils are the mark of a sophisticated bar.

 Vegetable peeler. Use a vegetable peeler when you want the thinnest peels for your drinks.

Whisks and whips. These are mostly used for cream or coffee drinks.

Glassware: The Long and Short of It

A fine cocktail is as much a pleasure to behold as it is to drink. It is said that the champagne goblet was modeled on Marie Antoinette's breast. Glasses, like breasts, come in all shapes and sizes. Lead crystal, which possesses an almost lofty musical tone—and a price to match—should be your glass of choice. The best glasses are thin lipped yet have a substantial feel. Always choose a long-stemmed glass for cold drinks served without ice. As tempting as it may be to grab the bowl of a cocktail or other stemmed glass—or as necessary as it may be after imbibing several—the purpose of the stem is to keep body heat away from the beverage. Do not be seduced by colossal goblets just because they are fashionable: Keep in mind the effect of two Martinis and stick to the more traditional 4- or 5-ounce glass, which will ensure visual elegance and a clearer head.

Which glasses and how many should you buy? If you like to entertain but are on a budget, there are kitchenware stores to accommodate you. Always buy more than you need, because it is easier to go to your closet when one breaks than it is to head back to the store. Also, glasses go out of fashion, and your favorite may no longer be available. You should also have a special cache of glasses just for special occasions.

- **Beer mug, stein, and pilsner glass.** These glasses are popular for beer-based cocktails.

- **Brandy snifter.** This type of glass ranges from a small 4-ounce globe, which can fit neatly into the palm of the hand, to a balloon-sized, 24-ounce Goliath.

- **Champagne flute and glass.** The flute is favored over the saucer champagne glass because the former keeps the bubbles from dissipating too quickly.

Cocktail or Martini glass. Although Martinis have been around for more than a century, the familiar triangular glass shape did not come into vogue until the '50s. Prior to that, cocktail glasses came in all shapes and sizes, but they all had stems.

Collins or chimney glass. This is a tall, slim, frosted glass ideal for summer drinks.

Cordial glass. This glass, stemmed or not, is also called a "pony glass."

Highball glass. A standard for a traditional mixed drink, such as a Bloody Mary or a Gin and Tonic.

Irish Coffee mug. This glass, which has a handle, is used for all hot drinks.

Margarita glass. Although the Margarita may be served in any stemmed glassware, its popularity has generated festive, ample-bowled glasses specifically for this drink.

Old-fashioned or rocks glass. Also known as an "on-the-rocks glass," this glass can be straight sided or barrel shaped.

Pousse Café glass. This glass resembles a cordial glass, but it usually flares out slightly at the top.

Punch bowl and glasses. Usually sold in sets, these glasses and bowls range from simple, clear glass to elaborate cut crystal.

Sherry glass. This glass is ideal for apéritifs.

Shot glass. This glass will not vary beyond a 1- to 2-ounce capacity.

Sour glass. The slender sister to her brother, the cocktail glass.

Special glasses. These may include hurricane glasses, mugs, goblets, and the like.

Wine glass. Choose red or white wine glasses for frozen drinks.

Stocking the Bar

The first tier of this section includes spirits, garnishes, condiments, and mixers for a basic home bar. Adding the items in the second tier would produce a bar that Dean Martin and the Rat Pack would be proud of. Individual taste and price will dictate what you purchase, but always look for top-shelf brands. Bear in mind that the "proof" content of spirits is double the alcohol percentage: 80 proof is 40 percent alcohol.

FIRST TIER

1. Amaretto
2. Anisette
3. Bourbon
4. Brandy
5. Cognac
6. Cointreau or triple sec
7. Crème de menthe
8. Curaçao, blue and white
9. Gin
10. Grand Marnier
11. Kahlúa
12. Pernod or Ricard
13. Rum, white
14. Sambuca
15. Tequila, white
16. Vermouth, dry
17. Vodka
18. Whiskey: rye, Scotch, blended, and Irish

Garnishes and Condiments

1. Angostura bitters
2. Black pepper
3. Cocktail olives
4. Cocktail onions
5. Fresh fruit
6. Grenadine
7. Horseradish
8. Lemons
9. Limes
10. Maraschino cherries
11. Rose's Lime Juice
12. Salt
13. Superfine sugar
14. Tabasco sauce
15. Worcestershire sauce

Mixers

1. Bottled water
2. Club soda
3. Cola
4. Diet cola
5. Lemon juice, fresh
6. Lime juice, fresh
7. Lemon-lime soda
8. Milk
9. Mineral water
10. Orange juice
11. Tomato juice
12. Tonic water

SECOND TIER

1. Absente, Absinthe Refined
2. Amer Picon
3. Applejack
4. Aquavit
5. B & B
6. Bailey's Irish Cream
7. Beer, ale, and stout
8. Bénédictine
9. Byrrh
10. Cachaça
11. Calvados
12. Campari
13. Canadian whisky
14. Chambord
15. Chartreuse
16. Cherry Heering
17. Crème de banane
18. Crème de cassis
19. Crème de noyaux
20. Drambuie
21. Dubonnet
22. Fernet Branca
23. Framboise
24. Frangelico
25. Fruit-flavored brandies
26. Galliano
27. Irish Mist
28. Jägermeister
29. Kirsch, kirschwasser
30. Kümmel
31. Lillet
32. Maraschino liqueur
33. Midori
34. Pimm's No. 1
35. Rumple Minze
36. Sake
37. Schnapps: apple, peach, peppermint, and so forth

38. Single-malt Scotch
39. Sloe gin
40. Southern Comfort
41. Tequila, gold
42. Tia Maria

43. Tuaca
44. Vandermint
45. Vodka, flavored
46. Wine and port

Garnishes and Condiments

1. Bananas
2. Celery
3. Celery seeds
4. Cinnamon sticks
5. Cloves
6. Cucumber
7. Eggs (Note: Although salmonella from fresh eggs is relatively rare, especially in farm-fresh or organic eggs, you may want to boil them for one minute before using them in a drink.)

8. Ground cinnamon
9. Heavy cream
10. Light cream
11. Mint sprigs
12. Nutmeg
13. Orange bitters and Peychaud's Bitters
14. Pineapple
15. Strawberries

Mixers

1. Beef bouillon
2. Clamato juice
3. Coconut cream
4. Coffee
5. Cranberry juice
6. Ginger ale
7. Ginger beer

8. Grapefruit juice
9. Lemonade
10. Orange flower water
11. Orgeat (almond syrup)
12. Peach nectar
13. Pineapple juice

Technique: A Short Course in Mixology

With your bar stocked, your glasses sparkling, and your shaker in hand, you are ready for the adventure to begin. Of course, procuring all the fixings and equipment is only the first step. Now you will need some basic skills plus a few tips and tricks of the trade. Just as chefs set up their ingredients before cooking, what they call their *mise en place*, you should have your preparations all laid out and your basic bar techniques down. Follow the guidelines below, and you will be creating drinks—and smiles—in a relatively short time.

ICING

Ice was a precious commodity, available only to the rich, prior to the second half of the twentieth century. Even when it became widely available, there were no ice machines, and bartenders hacked at large ice blocks, breaking them into small chunks—hence the name "rocks." Home freezers were previously small or nonexistent, and ice simply was not as cold as it is today. We may take ice for granted, but it is an essential building block of almost every cocktail and must be regarded with the same care as the spirits. It is paramount that ice must always be clean and be kept away from any contaminating odors. The size of the ice also makes a big difference. Because there is more chilled surface to many little cubes than to one very large one, a drink will chill faster with smaller cubes. Unfortunately, the ice will also dilute the drink more quickly. Apart from cocktails that call for cracked or crushed ice, opt for medium-size cubes.

For the coldest cocktails, chill the glasses in the refrigerator for several hours before using them, and store Martini glasses in the freezer. In a pinch, you can always add ice and water to an empty glass to quickly chill it. To frost a glass, dip it in water and put it in the coldest part of the freezer.

SHAKING, STIRRING, AND ROLLING

The debate over shaking versus stirring was around long before James Bond uttered his immortal line. In all honesty, it really does not matter as long as the drink is well mixed and ice-cold (as expressed by Lowell Edmunds in his classic book *Martini, Straight Up*). Although a consensus may never be reached on how to best serve a Martini or a Manhattan, some simple guidelines may be applied. Generally, any drink made with fruit juices, sugar, eggs, or cream should be shaken. Use a Boston shaker for this, and always add ice before the other ingredients. Hold the shaker well in front of you, then shake it vigorously in a diagonal motion. Most drinks need no more than ten seconds; after that, the shaking may dilute them. A small amount of melted ice, however, is a vital part of a shaken cocktail. Strain with a coil-rimmed strainer. If you have room, store the shaker in the freezer.

Those who favor stirring do so because they believe stirred drinks maintain their clarity. Even if shaking imparts a cloudiness to the cocktail, it soon dissipates and will not adversely alter the taste. When mixing cocktails in a pitcher, fill the pitcher halfway with ice and stir at least 20 times with a glass stirrer or bar spoon. Stir longer if you prefer a colder drink. Carbonated drinks, such as a Gin and Tonic, need only be stirred twice, in their glasses.

Rolling, a milder form of shaking, is used with tomato juice–based cocktails. Holding a Boston shaker at a slight angle, gently rotate the ingredients until incorporated. Shaking tomato juice too hard produces a curiously foamy concoction recalling low-budget horror flicks.

MUDDLING

Muddling is the mashing or grinding together of such ingredients as mint or limes in the bottom of a glass. This releases all the flavors and allows them to meld before you add the rest of the ingredients. You can purchase a wooden muddler from a specialty store, but the back of a large wooden spoon will do in a pinch.

POURING

It is a capital mistake to shake or stir a cocktail and then let it sit. Pour the drink immediately, and place any leftovers into a separate container to avoid dilution. Some people enjoy the "dividend" left in the shaker, but it is always best to mix a fresh batch rather than drink a diluted cocktail.

RIMMING

For Margaritas, gingerly dab the top outer edge of a glass with a piece of lime. Then turn the glass on its side, lightly sprinkle coarse salt over it while rotating the glass, and shake off any excess that may have fallen into the glass. Follow this procedure for all rimmed drinks.

GARNISHING
Fruit

For lemons and limes, wash and dry the fruit as you normally would, and slice the nubs off each end. Cut the fruit in half lengthwise; then cut each half lengthwise into three or four equal wedges, depending on the size of the fruit. Remove any seeds. Quarter the wedges crosswise for muddling. If you prefer wheels or slices to wedges, cut off the ends and thinly slice the fruit crosswise for whole wheels. Cut them in half for slices. You may refrigerate the fruit, covered, up to one day.

To make twists, start by cutting the ends off the fruit as described above. Using a sharp paring knife, carefully slice from top to bottom, creating 1/2-inch-wide strips of zest. Avoid cutting too much of the pith with the peel. Bear in mind that it is called a "twist" for a reason: Always twist the peel over the drink to release the essential oils directly into the drink. Do not smear the peel along the rim unless a recipe specifically calls for this. After a little bit of practice, you will also be able to dazzle your guests with a bit of pyrotechnics by using the combustible oil in the peel to flame it. Cut the peel into 1 1/2 by 3/4-inch ovals. Light a match and pick up the peel, holding it by the shorter sides between thumb and forefinger a few inches above the glass. Place the match between the peel and the drink, and snap the peel sharply backward so that the oil jettisons across the flame and into the drink.

You can vary the size of the peels depending on the effect you want. There is also a garnish called a "horse's neck." For this garnish, remove the ends of the fruit. Starting at the top, use a channel knife or a paring knife to cut one continuous 1/2-inch swath around the fruit.

Olives

The Martini is the exclusive province of the olive, and since the Martini is the paragon of cocktails, the olive is as vital to the bar as any ingredient. The goddess Athena is said to have presented the olive to ancient Greece, and it is difficult to imagine life—or the Martini—without it. But which olive? For sheer aesthetic appeal, some favor the pimiento-stuffed olive, while others shudder at the thought and advise using only a pitted green olive. Unlike a lemon peel, which imparts a particular flavor to the Martini, green olives are brined differently throughout the world and each type has its own flavor. For plain, whole green olives, French Picholine and Lucques are excellent, meaty choices. Greek Peloponnesian, Ionian, and cracked olives are also exceptional, as are any number of Californian varieties. Black olives are a definite no-no. Whether you prefer your olives soaked in brine or vermouth or stuffed with capers, jalapeño peppers, anchovies, or blue cheese is a matter of personal taste. But at all costs,

avoid olives packed in olive oil. You don't want an offshore oil slick floating atop your Martini.

JUICING

Always look for the juiciest of fruit. Size is not an indicator, but texture is.
The fruit should have some give when squeezed. Lemons or limes that
feel like baseballs will be mealy or pulpy. A good electric juicer or a metal
hand juicer is an ideal, and essential, tool. Fruit that is pliable and thin-
skinned is best for juicing. Roll it on a flat surface with the palm of your
hand prior to cutting to make juicing easier. Do not refrigerate the fruit,
but keep the juice in the refrigerator until ready to use it later the same
day.

SIMPLE SYRUP

Although superfine sugar can be substituted, simple syrup is an easy, con-
venient way to sweeten drinks without the granularity that may linger
from sugar. Combine 2 cups each of sugar and water in a small saucepan,
and cook over medium heat until the sugar dissolves. Let the mixture
cool, place it in a bottle with a drink pourer, and refrigerate it. Simple
syrup may be used wherever superfine sugar is mentioned in the recipes in
this book, but I have also indicated a substitution of simple syrup when a
truly smooth drink is desirable.

A Short Guide to Spirits

THE BASICS

Brandy

Brandy is the alcohol distilled from fermented fruit juices, including wine. Derived from the Dutch word *brandewijn*, meaning "burnt wine," brandy may be distilled from any fruit. The results are the myriad bases for countless varieties. Measuring in at around 80 proof, grape-derived brandies include cognac, Armagnac, grappa, and Jerez. Other fruit brandies derive their flavors from the fruit from which they are made, including apple, cherry, peach, and so on. Unlike other cocktails that require the best of spirits, you should never waste a fine cognac in a brandy drink—drink it straight.

Gin

In the middle of the seventeenth century, the Dutchman Franciscus de la Boë, professor of medicine at the University of Leyden, distilled spirits with *jenever*—juniper berries—for entirely medicinal purposes. When it reached England, it became known simply as gin. While some may argue that gin is still an effective medicine for what ails you, the British were producing it solely as a beverage by 1710. Cheap and easy to make, gin became so popular among England's poor people that the government attempted to curtail its production with the Gin Act of 1736. The response was similar to the reaction to Prohibition in the United States, inspiring such illicit varieties as Cuckold's Comfort and Royal Poverty.

At its core, gin is simply a neutral spirit distilled from grain. It is in the second distillation that gin gets its distinctive character. Botanicals such as juniper berries, anise, coriander, and potentially dozens of other herbs and spices impart their flavor to the spirit. The earliest gins, such as

England's Old Tom gin, were made with sugar. By the end of the nine-teenth century, unsweetened gin known as London Dry supplanted them and set the trend to come. A dry gin today is simply a gin that is not overly floral.

There is no one preferred gin, and a good home bar would do well to stock several. Dutch gin is heavy and complex, and at 70 to 80 proof it is generally drunk neat and very cold—and never in a Martini. English gins run the spectrum from bone-dry to refreshingly botanical, with a higher proof ranging from 86 to 94. The United States became a key producer of lower-proof, British-style gins, but the recent wave of smaller distilleries has also sired exciting new blends. France and Ireland also have many agreeable offerings. Gin does not need aging and may be drunk as soon as it is distilled—as it often was right out of the bathtub during Prohibition.

Rum

The derivation of the word *rum* is obscure. One theory is that it came from the Latin word for sugar, *saccharum*, but it may just as well have resulted from someone attempting to pronounce his own name after imbibing too much of this deceptively powerful liquor. Barbados and Puerto Rico both claim to have invented rum in the seventeenth century. Within a century there were nearly 160 distilleries in New England alone. Rumbullion or Kill Divill, as rum was called in colonial times, is made from sugar cane that is crushed, boiled down into molasses, fermented, and then distilled. All rum is aged for at least two and up to ten years, longer for añejo, or "aged" rum. Light (or silver) rum is clear, while medium (or gold) rum is slightly darker due to longer aging or the addition of caramel. Dark rum is the result of longer aging and more caramel, creating a heavier, more aromatic liquor. Modern distilleries are experimenting with the addition of spices and other aromatics. Last, there is the prodigious 151-proof rum, which could immobilize a fully grown elephant.

Tequila

Tequila's roots go back a thousand years to a cactus plant that served as the basis for *pulque*, a form of Mexican beer. The Spaniards distilled pulque in the sixteenth century to make tequila. A captain under Cortez, Bernal Díaz, crooned that it was a "nectar of the Aztec gods," which only proves that it takes more than nectar to keep your country from being conquered. To set the record straight, tequila is distilled only from the blue agave cactus plant. Mezcal, often bottled with its trademark agave worm, may be produced from any agave plant. At maturity, the plant is denuded of its prickly leaves, and the core of the plant is heated to extract the sap. The sap is then fermented, distilled, and ready for drinking. Aged tequila is stored in oak barrels that impart a golden color and delicate flavor to the tequila.

As late as 1968, Alec Waugh in his book *Wines and Spirits* declared: "Tequila is not a drink that is ever likely to be popular among North Americans, whose palates have not been hardened by the unrestrained use of chili." Moreover, it wasn't until 1975 that tequila was recognized by the U.S. Bureau of Alcohol, Tobacco, and Firearms as a distinctive product of Mexico. With a nod to the Margarita, tequila is now in the top ten best-selling spirits in the United States and is steadily gaining favor throughout the world. Hot on the heels of designer gins and vodkas, unblended "single-barrel" tequilas are now being distilled and sold for upward of $50 a bottle—without a worm.

Vodka

Consider a drink that is odorless, colorless, and tasteless, and water immediately comes to mind. But these characteristics are the legal restrictions put on vodka that is produced in the United States. Vodka, translated from Russian as "little water," produces massive profits for distilleries around the world. The Poles and the Russians both claim its birthright, and while its history there is legendary, its presence outside Eastern Europe was scarce up to the twentieth century. Rudolf Kunett (originally "Kunnetchansky") was a Russian émigré who bought the rights to produce Smirnoff vodka in the United States. Dismayed by poor sales, he sold the Smirnoff rights to Heublein president John Martin for $14,000 in 1939. The sale initially became known as Martin's Folly because of consumers' relative indifference to the product. Almost single-handedly, however, the astute executive reversed vodka's fortune—and his own—by tenaciously promoting it through such cocktails as the Bloody Mary, the Moscow Mule, the Screwdriver, and the Vodkatini (see "Vodka Martini"). The crisp, clean spirit was touted as a universal mixer that would also not leave a scent on your breath; even more of a selling point was that it would not result in a typical hangover the next day. Helped along by Ian Fleming's James Bond, Martin's vodka would become the most popular spirit in the United States and the second in the world, after rum, by the end of the twentieth century.

The simple reason for vodka's success is its amiability and chameleon-like nature—it blends with practically anything. Originally made from potatoes, vodka is distilled from fermented wheat, corn, or rye and is filtered through charcoal to remove any perceptible flavor. That said, the Russians, and subsequently nearly everyone else, have been adding flavors to vodka. Pepper, lemon, and various grasses have been added for centuries and have been joined today by every manner of berry and even vanilla. The potato is back, too, as evidenced by the Idaho Vodka Distillery.

Whiskey

To paraphrase an old song, "You say whiskey, and I say whiskey." But not everyone spells it the same. The Irish and American version is spelled "whiskey," while the Canadian and Scotch version is spelled "whisky." Now that that's out of the way, whiskey comes from the Gaelic translation for "water of life," *usqubaugh,* and has been made in Ireland and Scotland for at least seven hundred years. Whatever the spelling or pronunciation, all whiskey is created by a fermentation process similar to that of beer, but with an extra step: distillation. Grain is cooked in water to make a "mash," malt is added to produce sugar, yeast is then added to produce alcohol, and the alcohol is distilled from it. Whiskey is watered down to its appropriate proof, and the liquid is then aged in oak barrels.

American whiskey can be broken down into four types, which can be either straight or blended: bourbon, Tennessee whiskey, rye, and corn whiskey. Straight whiskey must be distilled from a mash of at least 51 percent of its base grain and diluted to no less than 80 proof. Blended whiskey combines at least two 100-proof whiskeys and other spirits. Bourbon, named for Bourbon County, Kentucky, is distilled from a mash of at least 51 percent corn stored in charred oak barrels. Tennessee whiskey is distilled just like bourbon but is filtered through sugar-maple charcoal before it is put into barrels. Rye must be distilled from at least 51 percent rye, often with a mix of corn and barley, but straight rye contains no other grains. Although rye was America's first whiskey, it is rarely seen anymore. Recipes like the Manhattan call for rye, not bourbon, and it is worth it to experiment with this subtle liquor. Corn whiskey is distilled from 80 percent corn, and, to quote the aptly named American wit Irvin S. Cobb, "it has the power to snap [a man's] suspenders and crack his glass eye right across."

Canadian whiskies are distilled from corn, rye, and barley. These blended whiskies are often generically, and mistakenly, called "rye." Generally lighter than American whiskey, they are aged for at least four years.

Irish whiskey is a hearty blended spirit made with grain and barley malt whiskeys. Said to have been invented by St. Patrick in the fifth century, Irish whiskey is strong, usually 86 proof, but not as smoky as Scotch whisky. This is because the malt in Irish whiskey is dried in coal-fired kilns, where it does not come in contact with the smoke. Irish whiskey can only be produced in Ireland.

Scotch whisky is blended similarly to Irish whiskey, but the native barley is dried over open peat fires, producing its characteristic smoky flavor. A single-malt whisky is not blended and is entirely produced at a single distillery. There are roughly a hundred of these distinct distilleries in Scotland. Scotch whisky can only be produced in Scotland. This may seem obvious, but several spurious brands distilled elsewhere have included "Scotch" in their names.

THEIR COMPANIONS
Liqueurs and Apéritifs

A well-stocked bar of liqueurs, with its shimmering greens, red, and blues, is like a precious stained-glass window. Apéritifs are also known as cordials; although the former were once made from fruit and the latter from herbs, the terms are now interchangeable. Dating back to the bubbling brews of the Middle Ages, liqueurs are infusions, percolations, and distillations of fruits, herbs, and spices. Infusion is rather like making tea, where fruits are steeped in alcohol, almost always brandy, until the flavors are harmoniously united. *Percolation*, which is another name for "bubbling," pumps the spirits up over the herbs. Distillation by heat extracts flavors. Some liqueurs are made by all three processes. Among the most common liqueurs are amaretto, anisette, chartreuse, crème de cacao, crème de menthe, curaçao, kirsch, Sambuca, and triple sec (see "Stocking the Bar," page 15, for more information).

Apéritifs are mixtures of wine spirits and as many as forty different kinds of exotic spices, roots, herbs, and flowers. The very word, albeit French, is derived from the Latin *aperio*, meaning "to open up, to lay bare." Recipes dating back to ancient Rome and Greece used parsley, asparagus, or almost anything they could find to mellow strong wines. The American plains dwellers mixed water with buffalo gall and, of course, whiskey. It should also be noted that, strictly speaking, vermouth, which is a fortified wine, is an apéritif.

Field Guide to Cocktails

A rose may be a rose, but a Danish Mary is a Hamlet's Ghost—which is to say, the same cocktail may go by a number of different names. For that matter, the Danish Mary is a variation on the classic Bloody Mary. In this guide, parent cocktails are grouped with their offspring as much as possible, and according to this system, the Danish Mary and the Hamlet's Ghost will be found under one entry. Conversely, there are cocktails that are seemingly alike but that are actually worlds apart. Although most variations on the Martini appear under the original gin-based cocktail, the Vodka Martini is a species in itself, deserving of its own entry. There are also category entries for bourbon, gin, apéritifs, flips, and so on, for more generic recipes. Recipes specifically referenced in other recipes appear in boldface type at their first mention. Cocktail-related books mentioned throughout are listed in the bibliography.

Note: Generally speaking, all cocktails containing less than 4 ounces are short drinks, whereas tall drinks, or long drinks, contain at least 6 ounces. Each cocktail includes a main recipe accompanied by an icon suggesting the glass in which it should be served. Other recipes may follow, along with appropriate variations. The recipes make one drink unless otherwise specified. Feel free to multiply the recipes accordingly.

1.   **ABSINTHE**

General
Description:

Absinthe is a strong herbal liqueur distilled with many flavorful herbs, including anise, licorice, hyssop, veronica, fennel, lemon balm, angelica, and wormwood. Although true absinthe is illegal, contemporary manifestations, which have an anise flavor, are quite popular. Every historian of nineteenth-century literature and art knows that absinthe was a veritable poison. This dazzling green liqueur was the signature drink of famous artists, writers, and poets: Picasso, Hemingway, Manet, Toulouse-Lautrec, and Oscar Wilde all heavily indulged in it. The "green fairy" was said to inspire their creativity, but because of the lethal component wormwood, it was also habit-forming and hallucinogenic; it incited heavy absinthe users to madness and suicide. Wormwood had been used medicinally since the Middle Ages, primarily to exterminate tapeworm infestations while leaving the human host uninjured and even rejuvenated, which is to say "stoned."

It should come as no surprise that one of the most popular alcoholic beverages in the world, bottled between 120 and 150 proof, was banned in the U.S. in 1915. Not content to let a good thing go, tipplers have been experimenting ever since with varieties of liquors and mixers to attain the same blissfully snookered state. Pastis (from the French *pastiche*, meaning "hodgepodge") can be any number of modern anise-flavored liqueurs that have supplanted absinthe.

Purchase:	Chief among the absinthe substitutes is the anise-flavored Pernod, a brand of pastis. Absente, Absinthe Refined, a modern version of the original absinthe recipe using a less bitter cousin botanical, southern-wormwood, is also widely available. Absente also comes with an actual, gratis slotted absinthe spoon on the box. Good luck finding Absente in your local pub.
Areas and Time of Occurrence:	The French are quite specific as to the time to imbibe absinthe. They have referred to it as *l'heure vert*, "the green hour." When exactly this is, however, has never been made clear. Donning a beret and discussing existentialism at an outdoor café under a setting summer sun would provide a very absinthe moment.
Season:	The young French poet Rimbaud wrote a series of poems entitled "A Season in Hell." As you might expect, there weren't many laughs in it. And neither are there many laughs in authentic absinthe—unless you get a kick from madness and suicide. Pastis and the other forms of modern absinthe, however, are happily, and safely, enjoyed throughout the year.
Preparation:	This drink was traditionally served with cold water and a cube of sugar, because absinthe was very bitter. The sugar was placed on a decorative, nearly flat, slotted absinthe spoon, and water was drizzled over it into the glass, turning the liquid a milky greenish white (the effect is called "louche"). Absinthe-type

cocktails are becoming quite popular. You should use a slotted absinthe spoon to simulate the original, but a silver tea strainer will work just as well.

Flavor
Affinities:

Since one rarely settles for a single serving of these drinks, choose savory and filling foods, such as mussels, pâté, and cheese with good French bread.

Recipes:

Absinthe Drip:
2 ounces Absente or anise-flavored liqueur
1 sugar cube
Ice water to taste

Pour the spirits over crushed ice in a chilled glass. Place the absinthe spoon across the rim of the glass, and place the sugar cube in the bowl of the spoon. Slowly drip the water over the sugar to melt the sugar into the glass. Do not stir, as this will diminish the aesthetic.

Absinthe Suissesse:
1¹/₂ ounces Absente or anise-flavored liqueur
3 dashes of anisette
3 dashes of orange flower water (available in specialty stores)
1 teaspoon white crème de menthe
1 egg white
Pinch of orange zest

Shake the Absente, anisette, orange flower water, crème de menthe, and egg white well with ice to emulsify the egg. Strain into a chilled cocktail glass, and garnish with a pinch of orange zest.

2.   **ADONIS**

General
Description:

The Adonis is a simple, low-alcohol, sherry-based cocktail. In its original form, the Adonis is a wine cocktail that dates back to the late 1800s. The name is derived from an 1884 play about a gorgeous male statue that comes to life and finds human ways so unpleasant that he willingly turns back into stone. *Adonis* was the first Broadway play to run for more than five hundred performances, but despite its lineage, the Adonis cocktail is rarely seen anymore and has entered the endangered species list. Bartender extraordinaire Dale DeGroff has attempted to revive it with his variation, the Adonis 11, at New York's Rainbow Room.

Purchase:

You could order this from Gary Regan at the old-world-style Pete's Tavern in New York, but since most other bartenders will probably give you a sly look when ordering an Adonis, try making this at home.

Areas and Time
of Occurrence:

One would imagine that the Adonis was served in drawing rooms at refined afternoon gatherings or after amateur music or dance recitals. You may want to serve it after paying a fortune to see a modern play that nearly turned you to stone.

Season:

Being a relatively mild cocktail, the Adonis is a perfect year-round drink.

Preparation:

A basic shaker or cocktail pitcher is all that is needed for the Adonis.

Flavor Affinities:

The Adonis is a graceful transmutation of a simple glass of sherry and would be suitably accompanied by tea cakes or cucumber sandwiches.

Recipes:

Adonis:
1 teaspoon bitters
³/₄ ounce sweet vermouth
1¹/₂ ounces dry sherry

Shake or stir all ingredients with ice; then strain into a chilled cocktail glass.

Adonis Cocktail:
(adapted from Dale DeGroff)
1 ounce sherry
1 ounce sweet vermouth
1 ounce fresh orange juice
Dash of Angostura bitters
¹/₂ teaspoon superfine sugar or simple syrup
Twist of orange peel

Shake or stir the sherry, vermouth, orange juice, sugar, and bitters with ice; then strain into a chilled cocktail glass. Garnish with orange peel.

Variation: **Bamboo:**
    Substitute dry vermouth for the sweet vermouth in the Adonis.

3a–c.   **ALEXANDER**

General
Description: *The Alexander is essentially a fortified dessert drink made chocolaty with dark crème de cacao (pronounced "ko-ko," not "ka-cow").* The Alexander is favored by those who want the "buzz without the bite." Because of its silken, refreshing creaminess, the Alexander is also known as a Milk Shake. Most people immediately associate brandy with the Alexander, but the earliest versions were made with gin. Despite its wide popularity, its origin is unknown.

Purchase: As a social drink, the Alexander is best ordered as a postprandial in lieu of straight brandy or cognac. When ordering out, be precise. A traditionalist may serve you a gin version.

Areas and Time
of Occurrence: Those who have soured on warm milk as an introduction to dreamland have taken to the Alexander as a nightcap. It is also favored throughout the evening by

those with a sweet tooth. But be careful with this one as well as with all warm-weather refreshers! Drinks like the Alexander invite you to indulge copiously and then suddenly pummel you into insensibility. John Lennon and Harry Nilsson were booted out of the Troubadour Club in Los Angeles as a result of their antics after imbibing a vat too many.

Season: The Alexander is generally ordered after meals in the warmer months.

Preparation: The Alexander is usually served in a cocktail glass, but larger cordial glasses also work nicely. It becomes a *Frappé* if you serve it over crushed ice in an old-fashioned or frappé glass. You may also skip the cream and ice and blend the alcohol with vanilla ice cream.

Flavor Affinities: The Alexander is a dairy dessert in a glass and would be best accompanied by nondairy cake or cookies.

Recipe: **Brandy Alexander:**
1 ounce brandy
1 ounce dark crème de cacao
1 ounce heavy cream
Pinch of freshly grated nutmeg

Shake the brandy, crème de cacao, and cream with ice; then strain into a chilled cocktail glass. Garnish with a pinch of nutmeg.

Variations: **Alexander's Sister:**
               Substitute crème de menthe for the crème de cacao.

               Gin Alexander:
               Blend equal parts gin, white crème de cacao, and
               heavy cream.

               Parisian Blond:
               Blend equal parts rum, curaçao, and heavy cream.

               Velvet Hammer:
               Substitute triple sec for the brandy.

4. ALGONQUIN

General   *This whiskey-based cocktail is rounded out by the tart-*
Description: *ness of pineapple juice.* Following the original recipe,
                which calls for rye whiskey, would put the Algonquin
                on the endangered species list, but most recipes these
                days call for blended whiskey. Named for the
                Algonquin hotel in New York, second home to such
                Round Table luminaries as Dorothy Parker, Robert
                Benchley, and Alexander Woollcott, the Algonquin
                brims with the sophisticated but tart edge of the pun-
                gent wits of the pre-Depression era.

Purchase: Having fallen out of fashion, the Algonquin is an "old
                newcomer" that may be unfamiliar to bartenders.

Areas and Time of Occurrence:	Since the members of the Round Table gathered for the ritual meetings during lunch, the Algonquin should be savored in the afternoons as a break from the midday doldrums or at a book club meeting to stimulate those little gray cells.
Season:	Whenever the world seems to be a little more ordinary and humdrum than usual, or when a siege of sadness sets in, shake up a batch of Algonquins.
Preparation:	Mix an Algonquin in a vintage cocktail shaker from the 1920s, and in no time you will be saying things like, "That woman speaks 18 languages and can't say no in any of them." A chilled cocktail glass is ideal for an Algonquin, but you may also serve it over ice in an old-fashioned glass for a longer drink. Straight rye is preferable to blended in this recipe.
Flavor Affinities:	Judging from the wits who indulged in the Algonquin, a serving of hot tongue was probably the order of the day. Today's tastes may lean toward a club sandwich or ham on "wry."
Recipe:	***Algonquin:*** **2 ounces straight rye or blended whiskey** **1 ounce dry vermouth** **1 ounce unsweetened pineapple juice** **Maraschino cherry**

Shake the rye, vermouth, and pineapple juice with ice; then strain into a chilled cocktail glass. Garnish with a maraschino cherry.

5.   **AMERICAN BEAUTY**

General
Description:

The concept behind the American Beauty is to create a cocktail as pleasant to look at as to sip. Whereas some cocktail names are straightforward descriptions of their contents, others are poetic invocations. Some of the latter border on the ludicrous or just meaningless (**Flirting with the Sandpiper**, anyone?), but—inspired by the American Beauty rose—this lush pink cocktail is a shimmering example of a perfectly named drink.

Purchase:

With the rising popularity of drinks like the **Cosmopolitan**, the rosy American Beauty is also finding favor with a young public interested in the seductive appearance of their drinks.

Areas and Time
of Occurrence:

The American Beauty is not a drink you should expect to find in lounges with cardboard ashtrays, shag-carpeted walls, and red vinyl bar stools. Think posh on this one. This potation is a black tie and slinky gown affair.

Season:

The optimal time of year to savor this cocktail is during the spring, the idyllic season when the rose of the same name is in bloom. Of course, keep in mind you can also buy a dozen of the roses at any time of the year at the local supermarket.

Preparation: The blend of numerous spirits in an American Beauty requires using a sturdy shaker and shaking vigorously. Although port is added at the end to simulate a red rose petal, bartenders have been known to drop actual petals into the cocktail. For a slightly sweeter drink, add a dash of simple syrup.

Flavor
Affinities: Prepare an intimate sundown garden party with hot and cold hors d'oeuvres, canapés, tartlets, and small quiches. All of these can be bought prepackaged.

Recipe: ***American Beauty:***
1 ounce fresh orange juice
1 tablespoon grenadine
1 ounce dry vermouth
1 ounce brandy
$1/4$ teaspoon white crème de menthe
$1/2$ ounce port
Rose petal (optional)

Shake the orange juice, grenadine, vermouth, brandy, and crème de menthe with ice; then strain into a chilled cocktail glass. Top with the port, and garnish with a rose petal, if desired.

6.   **AMERICANO**

General
Description:

Campari and vermouth are the elemental components of an Americano. The recipe for the Americano dates back to at least 1861, when it was served at Gaspare Campari's bar in Milan, a meeting place over the years for a variety of celebrities, from Giuseppe Verdi to Ernest Hemingway. It wasn't until Prohibition, with Americans flocking to Italy for a temporary reprieve, that the drink found favor with the visitors and was dubbed the Americano or the American Highball. Since the extremely bitter Campari was classified as a medicinal product in the United States, Americans took the recipe home, legally indulging throughout Prohibition. Occasionally referred to as a neutered **Negroni**, the Americano has found its admirers in the oddest places. In *A View to a Kill*, Ian Fleming writes, "No, in cafés you have to drink the least offensive of the musical comedy drinks that go with them, and Bond always had the same thing, an Americano."

Purchase:

You are more likely to find this drink at continental cafés and restaurants. The Americano is also a very simple, refreshing apéritif that is easily made at home.

Areas and Time
of Occurrence:

Order the Americano at an outdoor café under the stars, and imagine you are in Venice—unless you are already in Venice.

Season:

As a long drink, the Americano is suitable for an evening in early spring through late summer. With just a hint of soda, the Americano becomes a short drink that may be served as an apéritif year-round.

Preparation:

Most apéritifs are served in long-stemmed glasses, but since the Americano is considered a highball, a highball glass is the obvious choice. Put on the soundtrack to *The Talented Mr. Ripley* and start pouring.

Flavor
Affinities:

The pronounced tartness of the Americano cries out for the crunch of lighter antipasti, such as zucchini crisps, pizzettes, or batter-fried squash blossoms.

Recipe:

Americano:
1¹/₂ ounces Campari
1¹/₂ ounces sweet vermouth
Cold club soda
Slice of orange, lemon, or lime

Pour the Campari and vermouth over ice in a glass; then fill with club soda. Garnish with a slice of orange, lemon, or lime.

7.

AÑEJO HIGHBALL

General
Description:

The Añejo Highball is a complex, rum-based cocktail.
A new classic cocktail created by Dale DeGroff, a

recognized genius and craftsman among bartenders, as a tribute to the great bartenders of Cuba, the Añejo joins all three of the "holy trinity" of rum drinks through a blend of curaçao, lime, and rum. It epitomizes the bartender's creative art.

Purchase:

The Añejo is well on its way to becoming a classic cocktail, but it is still only to be found in the more chic and hip bars and nightspots. True to a great cocktail, it is relatively easy to make at home, following the recipe carefully.

Areas and Time
of Occurrence:

☾

If you live in or have the chance to visit New York City, order an Añejo at the Rainbow Room just before sunset and watch the Manhattan skyline slowly transform and intensify before your eyes.

Season:

☼

DeGroff intended the Añejo to evoke the "spiciness" of the Caribbean, and of Havana in particular, during the 1920s and 1930s. This cooling cocktail tames the torrid days of summer while kindling passions within.

Preparation:

Measuring and playing with recipes is not uncommon—and is often welcome. But the Añejo is one cocktail that cannot be improved upon. Añejo rum is a golden blend of rich, aged rums with a mellow taste and rich aroma. The name is derived from an ancient Spanish word meaning "aged."

Flavor
Affinities:

Any number of shrimp or fried oyster appetizers would go splendidly with the Añejo. For a Cuban flair, try making *bocaditos* (little party sandwiches) or a fish tartare.

Recipe:

Añejo Highball:
(adapted from Dale DeGroff)
1¹/₂ ounces añejo rum
¹/₂ ounce curaçao
2 ounces ginger beer
2 dashes of Angostura bitters
Orange and lime wheels

Pour the rum, curaçao, and ginger beer into a highball glass with ice cubes. Add the bitters, stir, and garnish the rim with the fruit.

8a–e.

APÉRITIF COCKTAILS

General
Description:

Apéritif cocktails are blends of wine, spirits, and liqueurs that are served generally before, but sometimes after, dinner. The cocktail may often be taken for granted, but the apéritif rarely is. Put the two together, and you have a sublime combination that beckons the appetizer tray. Whatever the ingredients, an apéritif is a light alcoholic beverage meant to stimulate the appetite, the conversation, and the mind. The soul of the apéritif is a mix of conviviality and reflection. Strictly speaking, the apéritif is a single spirit, such as Amer Picon or Lillet, but the recipes listed below are for apéritif cocktails.

Purchase:

With the dozens of apéritifs available today, you should think of Cole Porter's words when considering what to order: "Experiment! Make it your business night and day." Practically every café or lounge will have its specialties, and there is no reason why you should not dabble in your own at home.

Areas and Time of Occurrence:

Strictly speaking, a cocktail is not meant to be an appetite enhancer. Most apéritifs, however, are sipped and savored before dinner to stimulate the appetite.

Season:

Seated on a deck overlooking the shore, watching people from a tiny café on a busy street, or camped before a blazing winter fire—you will find that all seasons are conducive to the apéritif cocktail.

Preparation:

Shaken or stirred. Cocktail glass or wine glass. The methods and presentations are as varied as the drinks.

Flavor Affinities:

Depending on the country of origin for the foundation of your cocktail, food possibilities are limitless, but keep them within moderate proportions. Trays of good olives, paper-thin prosciutto, roasted peppers, garlic sausage, and marinated mushrooms are all fine choices.

Recipes: ***Amer Picon Cocktail:***
2 ounces Amer Picon
1 teaspoon grenadine
1¹/₂ ounces fresh lime juice

 Shake all ingredients with ice; then strain into a
chilled cocktail glass.

French Kiss:
1¹/₂ ounces sweet vermouth
1¹/₂ ounces dry vermouth
Twist of lemon peel

Pour both vermouths into a chilled old-fashioned
glass with ice cubes. Garnish with lemon peel.

Kir:
1 tablespoon crème de cassis
6 ounces dry white wine
Twist of lemon peel

Pour the crème de cassis and wine into a chilled wine
glass with ice, stir, and garnish with lemon peel.

Lillet Cocktail:
1¹/₂ ounces Lillet
1 ounce gin
Twist of lemon peel

Stir the Lillet and gin in a pitcher half full of ice, and strain into a chilled cocktail glass. Garnish with lemon peel.

Seething Jealousy:
1 ounce sweet vermouth
¹/₂ ounce Scotch
¹/₂ ounce cherry brandy
¹/₂ ounce fresh orange juice

Shake all ingredients with ice; then strain into a chilled cocktail glass.

9a–b.

APPLEJACK

General
Description:

Applejack cocktails were originally made from the uniquely North American potable applejack, an 80- to 100-proof brandy aged for two years in wood. One might speculate why the applejack cocktail is on the endangered species list, particularly with apple-flavored cocktails so common. The reason is that the majority of modern apple cocktails are made from apple-based spirits other than applejack. The French apple brandy Calvados is a subtle, fruity breed by comparison. Unlike aged apple brandies, this white lightning is produced by a process known as "jack-ing," in which cold temperatures work to separate the water and alcohol by taking advantage of their different freezing points. The water freezes into ice and is strained out of the mixture while the ethyl alcohol remains liquid, resulting in a higher alcohol concentration. Applejack was an old standby of the early colonists and, also known as "Jersey Lightning," was favored during Prohibition for its comparative ease of home brewing. A local affectionate name in New England for applejack was "essence of lockjaw."

Purchase:	With relatively few true brands of the potent applejack on the market, you are more likely to order a drink that uses apple brandy or schnapps. Barring your own home distillation, seek out real applejack to sample in the recipes below at home.
Areas and Time of Occurrence:	With a true applejack drink at your side, you would most likely clean a musket on a dusty front porch with your hunting dog, Blue, snoring by your side.
Season:	Applejack will just about knock you on your keister at any time of the year.
Preparation:	Stir in a clean paint can with a stick if a shaker is unavailable.
Flavor Affinities:	Salted nuts or thick-cut potato chips will cut the tartness of the applejack cocktails, but pork and beans straight from a can will also do in a pinch.

Recipes: ***Applejack Cocktail:***
2 ounces applejack or apple brandy
¹/₂ ounce curaçao
2 dashes of Angostura bitters
Apple slices

Shake the applejack, curaçao, and bitters with ice; then strain into a chilled cocktail glass. Garnish with apple slices.

Jack Rose Cocktail:
1 ounce fresh lemon juice
¹/₂ ounce grenadine
2 ounces applejack

Shake all ingredients well with ice; then strain into a cocktail glass or serve over ice.

10.   **APRICOT COCKTAIL**

General
Description: *Among fruit-based brandies, apricot brandy is one that happily combines with a variety of juices and spirits.* Because of its subtle complexity, apricot brandy has been used as the basis for a number of Apricot Cocktails. The most popular, and most straightforward, is a simple but elegant mixture of lemon juice, orange juice, and gin, although vodka may be used.

Purchase:	With the numerous apricot brandies available, you will need to try several to see which you like best.
Areas and Time of Occurrence:	If you are ever sitting at a sushi bar puzzling over the menu, mulling things over with an Apricot Cocktail is a fine choice.
Season:	The Apricot Cocktail is a perfect all-season predinner drink. It mellows the mood while refreshing the palate.
Preparation:	You will want to use an all-metal shaker for the Apricot Cocktail to get it as cold as possible. This is a drink that you may want to experiment with, since its proportion of spirits is a question of individual taste.
Flavor Affinities:	Highly seasoned dishes such as Greek *meze*, Spanish tapas, and Chinese dim sum play well with this drink.
Recipe:	***Apricot Cocktail:*** **1¹/₂ ounces apricot brandy** **³/₄ ounce fresh orange juice** **³/₄ ounce fresh lemon juice** **1 ounce gin or vodka** **Maraschino cherry (optional)**

Shake the brandy, orange juice, lemon juice, and gin well with ice; then strain into cocktail glass. Garnish with a maraschino cherry, if desired.

11.   **AVIATION COCKTAIL**

General
Description:

The Aviation Cocktail is a gin-based cocktail whose special appeal comes from the addition of maraschino liqueur. Previously headed for the endangered species list, the Aviation Cocktail seems to be having a revival thanks to the Internet. The Aviation was once regarded as the prince of cocktails, but the scarcity of maraschino liqueur nearly sent the drink into tippler's oblivion. The name of this feisty Depression-era cocktail is supposedly linked to air travel of the time—a risky venture not for the faint of heart.

Purchase:

Only the most traditional or serious bars still make the Aviation. This is one drink that home-bartending aficionados are dabbling in.

Areas and Time
of Occurrence:

Classic haunts like the Savoy in London or Rainbow Room in New York are where you will find the Aviation Cocktail. Gents, if you do find yourself at the Rainbow Room without a jacket, they will provide one. It will no doubt be ill-fitting at first, but two sips of an Aviation will soon have you feeling as well dressed as Astaire.

Season:

This drink is worthy enough to fly in any season.

Preparation:

Shake the Aviation hard enough that tiny flecks of ice float in the drink as soon as it is poured. Stay clear of

the gooey syrup in maraschino cherry jars. It's no substitute for the liqueur.

Flavor
Affinities:

To go with this old classic, try some old favorites,
such as shrimp cocktail or deviled eggs.

Recipe:

Aviation Cocktail:
1¹/₂ ounces gin
³/₄ ounce maraschino liqueur
³/₄ ounce fresh lemon juice
Maraschino cherry (optional)

Shake the gin, maraschino liqueur, and lemon juice
well with ice; then strain into a cocktail glass. Garnish
with a maraschino cherry, if desired.

12.

BACARDI COCKTAIL

General
Description:

The Bacardi Cocktail is a classic blend of Bacardi light
rum with a hint of fruitiness and sweetness. Considered
a sophisticate's drink from its onset, the Bacardi
became particularly fashionable during Prohibition
among those who could afford to travel to hot spots
like Havana. The Bacardi Cocktail made with any
number of other brands was so popular in nightclubs
and bars in the 1930s that Bacardi went to the New
York Supreme Court to sue so that no other rum
could be used in making this cocktail. Bacardi won,

but it is not recorded how New York's finest upheld the ruling. Over the years, bartenders across the globe have come up with many successful variations.

Purchase: Most well-established bars will be delighted to make a Bacardi Cocktail for you, but it is also easily made at home.

Areas and Time of Occurrence: The Stork Club would have been the ideal venue at which to order a Bacardi Cocktail. Sadly, this celebrated posh New York nightclub closed in 1965. The drink has since taken on more of a tropical bent, and sunny, open-air bars like the one at Trader Vic's are well-disposed to the Bacardi Cocktail.

Season: When other drinks seem too harsh or just plain plebeian, order a Bacardi Cocktail.

Preparation: This is a short drink, and an all-metal shaker as well as a smaller cocktail glass should be used.

Flavor Affinities: Select light and savory fare to go with a Bacardi Cocktail. You may also like to try fresh oysters and an assortment of fresh fruit.

Recipe: ***Bacardi Cocktail:***
1¹/₂ ounces Bacardi light rum
¹/₂ ounce fresh lime juice
¹/₂ teaspoon grenadine

Shake all ingredients well with ice; then strain into a cocktail glass.

Variation: **Robson:**

Substitute ¹/₂ ounce fresh lemon juice for ¹/₂ ounce of the rum.

13a–b.

BEER COCKTAILS

General Description:

Any beer mixed with practically anything would qualify here. Generally speaking, the beer cocktail—or, more apropos, the beer confabulation—was devised by a conspiracy of malefactors whose goal was to defile the palate. Granted, the Black Velvet, created to commemorate the death of England's Prince Albert in 1861, is one of the few exceptions, but the singular purpose of most of these mishmashes is to stave off sobriety as quickly as possible. If you seek incomprehensibility, temporary amnesia, and a bar floor for your bedding, a drink like the Boilermaker is for you.

Purchase:

Beer cocktails are catching on because they have recently been touted as a good marketing tool for bars that otherwise do not feature beer.

Areas and Time of Occurrence:

As beer cocktails continue to gain unprecedented popularity, even respectable bars are fixing them. The Brickskeller in Washington, D.C., serves more than a dozen concoctions; the Blow My Skull Off is certainly not to be missed.

Season: You are just as likely to find a beer cocktail at a summer brunch as at a fall picnic.

Preparation: If you know how to pour beer correctly, you pretty much have this down already. The Skip and Go Naked, an American frat house classic, is mixed in a garbage pail with a ski pole. Do not attempt to make a beer cocktail in the company of a beer purist unless you are trained in the martial arts.

Flavor Affinities: Beer nuts, pretzels, pork rinds, and other bar staples are mandatory.

Recipe: ***Black Velvet:***
6 ounces cold Guinness
6 ounces cold champagne

Pour both ingredients into a beer glass, but do not stir.

Beer Buster:
1¹/₂ ounces chilled vodka
2 dashes of Tabasco
1 bottle of beer

Stir the vodka and Tabasco in a chilled mug; then add the beer.

Variations: **Boilermaker:**

Pour a shot of Scotch into a mug of beer. Dropping the shot glass into the mug makes it a **Depth Charge**.

Skip and Go Naked:

Mix together however much beer, gin, grenadine, and lemon juice you have.

14a–b. **BEE'S KISS**

General Description: *The Bee's Kiss originally mixed honey with dark rum, but light rum seems to be favored today.* Harking back to the days of the speakeasy in the United States and the heyday of the Ritz Bar in Paris, the Bee's Kiss is a graceful drink that is gaining in popularity along with its cousin the Bee's Knees. Its name, derived from the poetry of Robert Browning, is a coy Victorian allusion to tickling your beloved with your eyelashes. Both drinks will tickle rather than sting (for the latter effect, see **Stingers and Other Beasties**).

Purchase: You may need to share the recipe when ordering, since the Bee's Kiss is only just becoming known again.

Areas and Time of Occurrence: The Bee's Kiss is an intimate drink and should be served wherever anyone would be ready to bestow or receive a passionate kiss, or at least have a cheek tickled by someone's eyelashes.

Season: Like fresh honey, the Bee's Kiss is most associated with late summer. It is considered by some to be an antidote to the dragging dog days.

Preparation: Use a Boston shaker to blend the ingredients fully.

Flavor
Affinities: Sample a fruit and cheese platter along with a Bee's Kiss.

Recipe: ***Bee's Kiss:***
$1^1/_2$ ounces light rum
1 ounce heavy cream
1 teaspoon honey
Freshly grated nutmeg

Shake the rum, cream, and honey well with ice; then strain into a chilled cocktail glass. Dust with nutmeg.

Variation: ***Bee's Knees:***
Substitute gin for the rum, and $1/_2$ ounce fresh lemon juice for the cream.

---

15.   **BELLINI**

General
Description: *The Bellini is a rich blend of peach purée and Prosecco, a sparkling, dry Italian wine.* Named for the Venetian painter Giovanni Bellini, the Bellini was created at Harry's Bar in Venice in 1948 by owner Giuseppe

Cipriani. This classic, refreshing drink was served only in the summer months during the time white peaches were available. The juice and pulp of the peaches were extracted through a sieve and blended with Prosecco. The rosy-colored elixir became a year-round drink once frozen peach purée became available.

Purchase: If Venice is not on your travel agenda, you can always visit any of the Harry Cipriani bars in New York for the perfect Bellini. You will want to stay for dinner, but you may need to sell your firstborn to do this.

Areas and Time of Occurrence: Sip a cooling Bellini on a sunny late afternoon in a quiet café or, better yet, in a cozy Italian restaurant before dinner, and you will be at one with the world.

Season: The Bellini is summertime itself.

Preparation: Frozen peach purée is difficult to find, so you may be limited to savoring a Bellini during the summer months, when fresh peaches are at their finest. Despite what others tell you, only use white peaches for a Bellini, or the color and taste will be off.

Flavor Affinities: For a taste of the Bellini as you might savor it at Harry's Bar, serve appetizers of prosciutto with figs or with mozzarella, and set out a plate of assorted imported olives.

Recipe: ***Bellini:***
          3 ounces Prosecco
          1 ounce frozen and thawed white peach purée,
          or fresh (see below)

Combine a ratio of three parts Prosecco to one part
purée in a well-chilled highball glass or champagne
flute.

Peach Purée:
(Serves 4)
1 pound white peaches
Simple syrup, as needed

Peel, pit, and purée the peaches in a food mill; then
strain through a fine sieve. Add simple syrup if the
fruit is too tart. Refrigerate until cool.

Variations: ***Tiziano:***
              Substitute good white grape juice for the peach purée.

Rossini:
Substitute strawberry purée for the peach purée.

16a–b.   **BLACK RUSSIAN**

General   *A Black Russian is an unlikely but thoroughly satisfying*
Description: *blend of vodka and Kahlúa coffee liqueur.* This cocktail

was created by the barman Gustave Tops, who worked at the Hotel Metropole in Brussels around 1950. He used to make this cocktail for the American ambassador Pearl Mesta, and he probably had no idea that the Black Russian would become a perennial favorite. It goes without saying that any cocktail with "Russian" in its name has vodka as a primary component.

Purchase:

If there is one drink that practically every bartender in the world knows, it is the Black Russian. Short of pouring equal shots of vodka and Kahlúa and drinking them, the Black Russian is one of the easiest drinks to mix at home.

Areas and Time of Occurrence:

Let's face it—you are not going to find someone sipping a Black Russian at steakhouses like the Palm or Peter Luger's while discussing a million-dollar advertising deal. You will only come upon this cocktail where the word *serious* is forbidden.

Season:

Black Russians are anywhere, anytime, casual, fun drinks for people who don't care if the world is going somewhere rather quickly in a hand basket.

Preparation:

Vodka + Kahlúa = Black Russian. Any questions? White and Black Russians are among the few drinks that benefit from the ice melting in them, so serve either in a nice, hefty old-fashioned glass.

| Flavor Affinities: | A Black Russian is food itself, particularly when adapted as a Chocolate Black Russian. |

Recipe: ***Black Russian:***
1 ounce vodka
1 ounce Kahlúa

Pour both ingredients over ice in a chilled old-fashioned glass.

Variations: ***White Russian:***
Add $1/2$ ounce cream and shake with ice.

Chocolate Black Russian:
Place the vodka, Kahlúa, and 2 scoops chocolate ice cream in a blender. Serve in a wine glass or champagne flute.

17. **BLOODY MARY**

General Description: *Originally a blend of primarily tomato juice and vodka, the Bloody Mary, or just the "Bloody," has since started to include ingredients as diverse as basil and roasted garlic.* Just as the tomato is one of the most fertile ingredients for cookery, tomato juice—and vodka—in the form of the Bloody Mary has been endlessly reinvented. One wonders why a recipe should be included here, since almost everyone already makes the best Bloody

Mary. Let us say it is for the sake of completeness, and for yet another definitive version.

Created by Fernand "Pete" Petiot of Harry's American Bar in Paris, the Bloody Mary was supposedly named for one Mary who spent long hours at the bar awaiting her lover. After Prohibition, Petiot went to New York to become head bartender at the Regis. Of course, vodka was not yet popular in the States, so gin was substituted. The Regis also thought the drink's name a bit grisly, and it was changed to the Red Snapper. As much as one may drink like a fish, however, few want a drink named after one (still, see **Fishtails**). It is unclear when the Bloody Mary came to be called for the eponymous English queen, Mary Tudor, but Ernest Hemingway, in typical bravado, boasted to a friend in a letter of 1947 that he brought the drink to Hong Kong in 1941, where it "did more than any single factor except the Japanese Army to precipitate the fall of that Crown Colony." The Bloody Mary did not enter its full phase of glory until several years later, when John Martin used it along with several other drinks to promote a relative newcomer to the American drinking scene—Smirnoff vodka. The rest is history and the future.

Purchase: The Bloody Mary will vary with every bar and bartender. When you find one you like, ask for the ingredients. It is also a drink the home bartender continually experiments with "the morning after."

Areas and Time
of Occurrence:

It is no secret that the Bloody Mary is the quintessential "hair of the dog that bit you" and is presumed to be an antidote to a hangover. Brunch is therefore the most common time to mix a batch of Bloody Marys, especially since you probably overslept breakfast. It is equally a stimulating predinner drink. You may as well bite the dog before it bites you.

As much as we emphasize that all drink mixtures should be made fresh, the Bloody Mary is one rare exception, but only during a particular instance—when traveling by plane. Since you may want an in-flight cocktail, the Bloody Mary will supply you with a much-needed stimulant while providing nourishment. A can of Bloody Mary mix will have to suffice.

Season:

As a pick-me-up, the Bloody Mary is virtually time-less and universally welcome.

Preparation:

Horseradish or no horseradish? Celery salt, seeds, stalk, or none? These are the questions. Whatever your choice, build your Bloody Mary fresh. Experiment with vegetable juice as an alternative to tomato. In the best of all possible worlds, New York barman Dale DeGroff may have the best solution: a Bloody Mary buffet. Set out a large pitcher of tomato juice and a cold bottle of vodka. Then place any ingredient ever used to concoct a Bloody Mary next to the two, and encourage guests to make their own. Note that the Bloody Mary is not a vegetarian drink, because

Worcestershire sauce has anchovies. Keeping that in mind, try a dash of clam juice.

Flavor
Affinities:

Depending on your intake the night before, the Bloody Mary is a suitable accompaniment to anything from croissants, ham, and eggs Benedict to lox, bagels, and cream cheese.

Recipe:

Bloody Mary:
2 ounces vodka
4 ounces tomato juice
1/2 teaspoon good horseradish
2 dashes of Worcestershire sauce
3 dashes of Tabasco sauce
Pinch of coarse salt or sea salt
Pinch of freshly ground pepper
1/4 ounce fresh lemon juice
Pinch of celery salt or seeds, crushed
Wedges of lemon and lime

Combine the vodka, tomato juice, horseradish, Worcestershire sauce, Tabasco sauce, salt, pepper, lemon juice, and celery salt in a Boston shaker over ice, and roll gently to blend. Strain over ice into a highball glass. Garnish with a wedge each of lemon and lime. If you are hungry, add a tender celery stalk.

Variations:

Bloody Bull:
Mix vodka with equal parts tomato juice and beef

bouillon. Prepare as above, omitting the salt and celery salt.

Bloody Caesar:

Substitute Clamato juice for the tomato juice, or mix tomato and clam juice.

Bloody Maria:

Substitute tequila for the vodka.

Bullshot:

Substitute beef bouillon for the tomato juice. Add only 1 dash each of Tabasco and Worcestershire.

Danish Mary (Hamlet's Ghost):

Substitute aquavit for the vodka, and caraway for the celery salt.

---

18. **BLUE BLAZER**

General
Description:

A literally fiery concoction, the Blue Blazer is a Scotch-based drink that is mellowed by honey. With the sole ingredients of Scotch, honey, and water, the Blue Blazer might strike one as being relatively easy to prepare—wrong! Invented by legendary bartender "Professor" Jerry Thomas in the 1800s, the drink is as sensational as it is dangerous. Named for the blue flame that emanates when the drink is lit, the Blue

Blazer evokes the prudent advice, "Kids, don't try this at home!"

Purchase:
If you see asbestos gloves at a bar, chances are the bartender has had some practice making this drink. If you insist on making it at home, proceed with great care and begin by practicing outdoors.

Areas and Time of Occurrence:
☽
Many skilled and daring bartenders who also have pyromaniac tendencies are willing to fire up a Blue Blazer. The mixing of this incendiary drink gives the impression of a flowing stream of flame that is all but lost if served in daylight.

Season:
❄︎ ❅
The Blue Blazer is perfect for toasting any special occasion, but it also makes for a warming and soothing cool-weather nightcap—or fireman's cap, as the case may be.

Preparation:
You will need two heavy, deep mugs or silver mugs with insulated handles. Practice pouring hot water from one mug to the other before embarking on any pyrotechnics. Pouring back and forth actually simulates a bellows, resulting in a growing fire. When you get the knack of this, try pouring in a dimly lit room (over a fire-resistant surface).

Flavor Affinities:
Any number of hot hors d'oeuvres provide a comforting match, so to speak. Baked oysters and mushrooms

or hot Gruyère and anchovy canapés are just two of
many possible suggestions.

Recipe: ***Blue Blazer:***
(Serves 2)
2 tablespoons honey
¹/₄ cup boiling water
5 ounces Scotch or Irish whiskey
Twist of lemon peel

Pour the honey and water into one mug, and stir
until the honey dissolves. Warm the whiskey in a
saucepan until hot, but not boiling, and add it to the
second mug. Light the whiskey with a match, and
carefully pour it into the first mug. Pour the flaming
liquid back and forth from mug to mug several times.
When the flame subsides, pour into clear mugs or
cut-glass goblets and garnish with lemon peel.

19a–c.

BOURBON COCKTAILS

General
Description:

*Bourbon, not to be confused with Tennessee whiskey
(page 27), is generally preferred neat or with a splash of
soda or "branch water."* The writer Walker Percy
declared, "Bourbon does for me what that piece of
cake did for Proust." The Mint Julep aside, most
bourbon recipes are variations on other drinks:
Collinses, Daisies, Slings, and so on. Following are

some distinctive bourbon recipes that stand apart. A number of recipes for bourbon are rye cocktails that have been converted to this more accessible spirit.

Purchase: If the adventurous drinker should happen upon a serious bartender, query him or her about unusual drinks made with bourbon. You never know what you might discover.

Areas and Time of Occurrence:

The world is your oyster. Shuck it.

Season: The ingredients of your cocktail will dictate the season to drink it.

Flavor Affinities: Bourbon has a subtle sweetness about it, and the foods you select should counterbalance that. Look for foods that tend to be salty or savory.

Recipes: **Brown Derby:**
This signature cocktail from the Vendôme Club memorializes the Brown Derby, the Wilshire Boulevard restaurant perhaps remembered more for its hat-shaped exterior than for the celebrities who frequented it.
2 ounces bourbon
1 ounce fresh grapefruit juice
1/2 ounce honey

Shake all ingredients well with ice; then strain into a chilled cocktail glass.

Horse's Neck:

The continuous spiral of orange peel (page 21) gives this drink its name.

1 horse's neck spiral of orange peel
2 ounces bourbon
4 ounces cold ginger ale

Drape the spiral around several ice cubes in a highball glass, and allow some excess peel to hang over the edge of the glass, simulating a horse's neck. Add the bourbon and ginger ale.

Bourbonella:

We may never know whether this nearly forgotten drink from the 1970s was named for the character Barbarella, but it is way out there.

2 ounces bourbon
1 ounce dry vermouth
¹/₂ ounce curaçao
¹/₂ ounce grenadine

Shake all ingredients well with ice; then strain into a chilled cocktail glass.

20a–c.   **BRANDY COCKTAILS**

General
Description:
Unlike bourbon, brandy, which is distilled from fermented fruit, is a natural mixer. Dr. Samuel Johnson said, "Claret is the liquor for boys, port for men; but he who aspires to be a hero must drink brandy." Given the innumerable kinds of brandies available, with new varieties appearing regularly, heroes must abound. As do brandy cocktail recipes. The more substantial recipes have been given their own entries, but here are a couple of old-timers with longevity.

Purchase:
Cocktail lounges are laboratories for brandy cocktails. Tell the bartender what your favorite brandies are, and get ready for the flavor of the week.

Areas and Time
of Occurrence:
Following Dr. Johnson's dictum, "hero time" would appear after hours, in all establishments—before, during, and after dinner.

Season:
Appropriate brandy cocktails exist for every subtle seasonal change of the year.

Flavor
Affinities:
When served before dinner, brandy cocktails pair well with savory dishes such as meat pies or mild salami. A platter of various cheeses would admirably suit these drinks after dinner.

Recipes: ***Brandy Crusta:***
Crustas go back to the end of the nineteenth century.
They are named for the sugar on the rim of the glass.
Sugar for rimming
2 ounces brandy
¹/₂ ounce maraschino liqueur
Dash of bitters
¹/₂ ounce triple sec or curaçao
¹/₂ ounce fresh lemon juice
Twist of lemon peel

Rim a chilled cocktail glass with sugar. Shake the
brandy, maraschino liqueur, bitters, triple sec, and
lemon juice well with ice; then strain into the glass.
Garnish with lemon peel.

Bosom Caresser:
2 ounces brandy
1 ounce Madeira
1 ounce curaçao
1 teaspoon grenadine
1 egg yolk

Shake all ingredients with ice; then strain into a
chilled wine glass.

Brandy Gump:
1¹/₂ ounces brandy
1 ounce fresh lemon juice

¹/₂ teaspoon grenadine

Shake all ingredients well with ice; then strain into a chilled cocktail glass.

21a–b.

BRONX COCKTAIL

General
Description:

The Bronx, or Da Bronx, is a gin-based drink that combines both sweet and dry vermouth and is enlivened by a splash of orange juice. In the 1930s, such a demand for the Bronx Cocktail existed at New York's Brass Rail in the Waldorf that the bar, under the tutelage of Johnny Solon, went through cases of oranges a day. The cocktail is named not for the much-maligned New York City borough but for the Bronx Zoo. One story has it that Solon visited the zoo and saw many strange beasts. Thinking that a number of his customers also saw bizarre beasties after too many drinks, he christened this cocktail the Bronx. As one might expect, Brooklyn got into the act with a cocktail of its own.

Purchase:

Bartenders who take pride in their mixology have tried to keep the Bronx alive, but it is mostly foreign to the new generation of barkeeps. This is a drink that can easily be made at home. If it is raining and wet, relax and order a Dry Bronx.

Areas and Time of Occurrence:	You will have about as much luck finding the Bronx at a bar as you would finding a Red Sox fan in the Bronx. Mix this one at home.
Season: 🌱 ☀ ❄ ❄	The Bronx, which has been as equally maligned as a drink as the borough has, will gratefully take any season you give it.
Preparation:	Some bartenders prefer to omit the orange juice. Our advice is to retain the OJ and get your vitamin C while preserving tradition. To avoid those many strange beasts that Mr. Solon referred to, keep your intake to no more than three. For a Sweet Bronx or a Dry Bronx, use only one kind of vermouth. If you replace the vermouth with a dash of bitters, the cocktail becomes an Abbey.
Flavor Affinities:	Although most tea sandwiches go down well with a chilled Bronx, a Danny Kaye favorite of parslied onion sandwiches would border on perfection.
Recipes:	***Bronx:*** **2 ounces gin** **¹⁄₂ ounce dry vermouth** **¹⁄₂ ounce sweet vermouth** **1 ounce fresh orange juice**

Shake all ingredients well with ice; then strain into a chilled cocktail glass.

Brooklyn:
2 ounces rye or blended whiskey
1 ounce dry vermouth
Dash of maraschino liqueur
Dash of Amer Picon

Shake all ingredients well with ice; then strain into a chilled cocktail glass.

22.

CAIPIRINHA

General
Description:

The Caipirinha is made with a base of cachaça, a five-hundred-year-old, sugar cane–derived spirit. Combine the popularity of the Martini and the Cosmopolitan, and you have Brazil's national drink—the Caipirinha, or Cachaça Sour. The Portuguese word politely translates as "little man from the country," or, less politely, as "yokel." The Caipirinha is drunk from lunch until bedtime, which may come sooner than anticipated. It has been popular throughout Brazil for longer than anyone can remember, which is not a surprise, given the potency of the drink and the frequency with which it is drunk.

Cachaça is a spirit akin to rum in that it is made from unrefined sugar, but the similarity stops there. Cachaça is a sharper, tart liquor that is tamed into seduction when muddled with lime and sugar.

| Purchase: | Bottles of cachaça are currently still difficult to obtain in many places, so the more upscale lounges and bars are the likely venues for ordering a Caipirinha. |

Areas and Time
of Occurrence:

As cachaça becomes more common, so will the appearance of the Caipirinha. Visitors to Brazilian restaurants, such as the famous *churrascarias*, or all-you-can-eat steakhouses, should take the opportunity to sample this cocktail. Since the Caipirinha is making its way into the chic bar scene, expect to pay much more for it at such establishments. Unlike drinks that are served as predinner or after-dinner fare, the Caipirinha seems to renew itself with each course.

Season:

Brazil, being consistently more temperate—if not downright more sultry—than other parts of the world, offers the ideal climate for sipping a Caipirinha and watching the rest of the world go by. The first warm days of spring through the end of summer are best suited for this refreshing drink.

Preparation:

The Caipirinha is a down-to-earth, honest drink that requires no ostentation. A good old-fashioned glass is all you need. The Caipirinha will do the rest. Until recently, only two brands of cachaça were generally available outside of Brazil: Pitú and Toucano. While not as complex, Pitú has a brashness and joviality that is more common to the Caipirinha found on the streets of Rio. Stick with regular granulated sugar, which will properly muddle the lime.

Flavor
Affinities:
The Caipirinha is a lively tart cocktail that goes well with savory appetizers such as empanadas, mushroom turnovers, sausages, and small trays of sharp cheeses and cold cuts. It also holds its own with such main courses as ceviche or the classic Brazilian black bean and meat stew, *feijoada*.

Recipe:

Caipirinha:
4 Key limes, halved and seeded, or two small, juicy
   limes, quartered
2 teaspoons granulated sugar
2 ounces cachaça

Sprinkle the sugar over the limes, and muddle them in the mixing glass part of a Boston shaker until the sugar is dissolved and the lime juice is released. Pour an old-fashioned glassful of cracked ice into the mixing glass, add the cachaça, and shake to incorporate. Return all the contents to the old-fashioned glass.

Variations:

Caipirissima:
Use rum in place of the cachaça.

Caipirosca:
Use vodka in place of the cachaça.

23a–d.

CAPE CODDER

General
Description:

*The Cape Codder initially combined equal parts vodka
and cranberry juice softened by sugar and water, but the
drink has evolved into a cranberry cocktail, eschewing
the sugar and water.* For one of the simplest and most
refreshing drinks around, nothing surpasses the Cape
Codder. Named for the area of Massachusetts where it
began as a bar special, the humble Cape Codder is a
perennial summer favorite.

On a historical note, the same fixings appeared in
a drink at Trader Vic's in the 1950s as the Rangoon
Ruby. It made a second appearance a decade later as a
Bog Fog. The Cape Codder has not only since held
its own but has inspired many variants.

Purchase:

Although a Massachusetts favorite, the easy-to-prepare
Cape Codder is beloved everywhere.

Areas and Time
of Occurrence:

By the sea, by the sea, by the beautiful sea . . . that is
the true home of the Cape Codder. When you cannot
be by the shore, a deck chair by the pool will suffice.

Season:

The Cape Codder travels well, and a thermos of this
ruby elixir is just as welcome at a lakeside barbecue as
it is at the shore at sunset.

Preparation:

The Cape Codder can be enjoyed freshly made or
stored in large batches ahead of time. Some variations

on the recipe call for light rum or applejack as the base, and some people add a touch of soda for an adult cranberry spritzer.

Flavor Affinities:
The Cape Codder is an all-time favorite at clambakes, but this summer treat also pairs well with anything from New England–style chips to a lobster dinner.

Recipe:
Cape Codder:
2 ounces vodka
5 ounces cranberry juice
Wedge of lime

Combine the vodka and cranberry juice over ice in a chilled highball glass. Garnish with a lime wedge.

Variations:

Bay Breeze:
Use 4 ounces unsweetened pineapple juice and 1 1/2 ounces cranberry juice.

Sea Breeze:
Use 4 ounces fresh grapefruit juice and 1 1/2 ounces cranberry juice.

Madras:
Replace 2 1/2 ounces of the cranberry juice with 2 1/2 ounces fresh orange juice, and garnish with a slice of orange.

24a–c. **CHAMPAGNE COCKTAIL**

General
Description:

The Champagne Cocktail is a marvelously simple mixture of champagne and a sugar cube soaked in Angostura bitters. This classic cocktail dates back to the Civil War era in the United States, when it appeared in Jerry Thomas's *How to Mix Drinks; or, the Bon Vivant's Companion.* The Champagne Cocktail was chosen by *Esquire* magazine as one of the top ten cocktails of 1934; although its popularity has waned, it still has unflagging adherents. For some sophisticates, it is still the only cocktail.

Purchase:

The inherent beauty of the Champagne Cocktail goes beyond its suave appearance and silken palate. Whereas you would expect to pay a goodly sum for an excellent bottle of champagne, the addition of the sugar and bitters nicely rounds out a less-expensive brand.

Areas and Time
of Occurrence:

A bottle of bubbly is universally recognized as the drink to celebrate happy events. Weddings, graduations, ringing in the New Year, and getting a raise are all times the Champagne Cocktail would serve as a delightful alternative.

Season:

Champagne knows no borders or time clock, and neither does the Champagne Cocktail.

Preparation: As much as you may want to commemorate Marie Antoinette's anatomy by serving in a goblet modeled after her breasts, a fluted glass preserves the effervescence. Remember, this is neither an Asti Cocktail nor a Cold Duck Cocktail. Champagne is a must.

Flavor Affinities: Joyous occasions deserve festive food. Caviar, pâté, or even crostini with tapenade (for those on a budget) would highlight this classic drink.

Recipes: ***Champagne Cocktail:***
1 dash of Angostura bitters
1 sugar cube
Cold, dry champagne
Twist of lemon peel

Add the dash of bitters to the sugar cube in the bottom of a chilled champagne glass, and slowly pour in the champagne. Garnish with the lemon peel.

Variations: ***Champagne Normande:***
Add a teaspoon of Calvados to the basic Champagne Cocktail recipe.

Kir Royale:
Add a splash of crème de cassis to a glass of champagne. The classic Kir is made with white wine.

Mimosa:
2 ounces fresh orange juice
4 ounces champagne

Pour the orange juice into a chilled champagne glass, and slowly pour in the champagne.

25a–e.   **CLOVER CLUB**

General
Description:

The Clover Club is a fruity mixture of gin, sweeteners, egg white, and nostalgia. For all intents and purposes, some drinks are dead, but no one has the heart to take them off the respirator. Like the epitaph on the atheist's grave, "All dressed up and no place to go," the Clover Club and other archaic cocktails are still noted, but few people know anything about their source.

The Clover Club has particularly suffered because of its name. Although it was supposedly named for a group of wits who roasted politicians once a year and tippled at the posh bar in the Bellevue-Stratford Hotel in Philadelphia, the name Clover Club reeks of some crummy dive where the whiskey starts pouring at nine in the morning. The drink, which dates from the late 1800s, was singled out by *Esquire* magazine in 1934 as one of the ten worst cocktails. In the spirit of raising Lazarus from the dead, however, the recipes for the Clover Club and several other cocktail cadavers have been resurrected below.

Purchase:	Historian and revivalist bartenders like Dale DeGroff and Gary Regan will know how to mix this cocktail, but only the most grizzled of other barkeeps will remember this relic.
Areas and Time of Occurrence:	Any number of people order a **Cosmopolitan**, others ask for a **Long Island Iced Tea**, and still others order Apple Martinis. This is the time to kick off the mothballs and order a Clover Club, and don't be surprised if everyone follows suit on the next round. Definitely do not order a Clover Club at a corner lounge called the Clover Club.
Season:	The Clover Club, the Pegu, and these other cocktails have had their season, which is not to say that you shouldn't give them a second chance.
Preparation:	As with all drinks mixed with eggs, the Clover Club must be shaken furiously. As a tip, don't tell anyone about the egg until after a few sips.
Flavor Affinities:	A Clover Club has a tartness that stands up to the bite of dishes such as escargot or spicy quail eggs.
Recipes:	***Clover Club Cocktail:*** 1¹/₂ **ounces gin** ¹/₄ **ounce grenadine** ³/₄ **ounce fresh lemon juice** 1 **egg white**

Shake all ingredients vigorously with ice for about 30 seconds; then strain into a chilled cocktail glass.

Honeymoon Cocktail:
³/4 ounce Bénédictine
³/4 ounce apple brandy
1 teaspoon triple sec

 Shake all ingredients with ice; then strain into a chilled cordial glass.

Maiden's Prayer:
1¹/2 ounces gin
¹/2 ounce fresh orange juice
¹/2 ounce fresh lemon juice
¹/2 ounce triple sec
Twist of lemon peel

 Shake the gin, orange juice, lemon juice, and triple sec with ice; then strain into a chilled cocktail glass. Garnish with lemon peel.

Pegu Club Cocktail:
2 ounces gin
¹/2 ounce blue curaçao
2 dashes of Angostura bitters
1 teaspoon fresh lime juice
Twist of lime peel

Shake the gin, blue curaçao, bitters, and lime juice with ice; then strain into a chilled cocktail glass. Garnish with lime peel.

Satan's Whiskers:
1 ounce gin
1 ounce fresh orange juice
¹/₂ ounce dry vermouth
¹/₂ ounce sweet vermouth
¹/₂ ounce Grand Marnier
Dash of bitters
Twist of orange peel

Shake the gin, orange juice, dry and sweet vermouths, Grand Marnier, and bitters with ice; then strain into a chilled cocktail glass. Garnish with orange peel.

26a–c.

COBBLERS AND FIXES

General Description:

In their earliest versions, cobblers and fixes were wine-based drinks shaken with ice. Over time, they have come to include any number of spirits and mixers served over crushed or cracked ice. The only real distinction is that a cobbler is 12 ounces and a fix, which appeared later in the twentieth century, is 8 ounces. While you may immediately associate the cocktail shaker with the Martini, it was the cobbler that truly heralded the advent of the modern shaker. By contrast, a fix is literally "fixed" in the glass. In his book *The Craft of the Cocktail*, Dale DeGroff points out that cobblers were initially shaken with fruit but that this technique passed out of favor by the 1930s, when fruit was added as a garnish. Stirring also replaced shaking. If you are in a hurry or simply in a quandary about what to mix in your cobbler, don't add anything. In this case, any straight liquor poured over crushed ice is called a "mist." For example, Midori over crushed ice is a Midori Mist.

Purchase:
The very elaborate cobblers and fixes, with their many flavorings and array of freshly cut fruit, are best ordered in a well-equipped lounge. With a little prep time and a little imagination, however, the home bartender can be stirring or shaking up cobblers or fixes with great ease.

Areas and Time of Occurrence:
Judging by how they are made in most bars these days, with glasses packed with crushed ice and spirits dribbled over, cobblers and fixes are something on the order of snow cones for adults. Their sunny disposition should be matched by the surroundings; these cool drinks are best suited to outdoor patio lounges or skylit bars bathed in sunlight.

Season:
The cobbler is a ubiquitous summertime favorite. For more seasonal cobblers, add locally fresh fruit.

Preparation:　Apart from being shorter than a cobbler, a fix also usually has a liqueur floated on top.

Flavor Affinities:　Cobblers and fixes are fruity and certainly varied. Match their diversity with a mixed bag of appetizers, such as Moroccan meatballs, smoked salmon roulades, and eggplant caviar.

Recipes:　***Basic Brandy Cobbler:***
1 teaspoon superfine sugar
3 ounces club soda
2 ounces brandy
1 ounce curaçao, kirsch, or other liqueur
Slice of orange, lemon, or other fruit

 Dissolve the sugar in the club soda in a chilled old-fashioned glass. Add cracked ice and the spirits. Garnish with pieces of your favorite fruit. Alternatively, muddle and shake and garnish with your fruit of choice.

Variations:　***Cherry Cobbler:***
Blend the sugar and soda with gin, cherry liqueur, and crème de cassis.

Rum Cobbler:
Use rum instead of brandy.

Irish Fix:
1 teaspoon simple syrup
2 ounces Irish whiskey
¹/₂ ounce fresh lemon juice
¹/₂ orange slice and ¹/₂ lime wheel
2 teaspoons Irish Mist

Add the simple syrup, whiskey, and lemon juice to a chilled highball glass. Fill with cracked ice, and stir well. Garnish with orange and lime, and float the Irish Mist on top.

27a–c. 📷　　**COOLERS**

General
Description:

Coolers are tall drinks or highballs that may include virtually any liquor. Another in the long line of summer drinks, coolers can be made with gin, rum, vodka, brandy, tequila, or whiskey. As varied as the ingredients, coolers have one goal in mixing—to be thirst-quenching and refreshing. Coolers are made with superfine sugar (or simple syrup) and club soda, although you may substitute ginger ale.

Purchase:　　Unlike the cobbler, the cooler demands no special prep work or dexterity. All one truly needs to prepare this most forgiving drink is a mighty thirst.

Areas and Time of Occurrence:	These tall drinks are just the ticket when you want to cool off on your porch and quaff something different from your usual rum and tonic.
Season:	When the heat of summer is upon you, an icy cooler is as welcome as a sudden, unexpected breeze.
Preparation:	Variations on coolers are as numerous as the steamy days of summer. About all you really need are ice cubes, chilled glasses, and a desire to cool off. If you happen to have any of those little floating drink holders shaped like Lifesavers, those would be perfect to float your cooler in the pool.
Flavor Affinities:	Fire up the barbecue grill or heat up a grill pan for a variety of Thai chicken, beef, or shrimp satay. Chips, crudités, and a blue cheese dip are other summer cooler pairings.
Recipe:	***Basic Cooler:*** **1 teaspoon superfine sugar** **Club soda or ginger ale** **2 ounces liquor of your choice** **Long lemon or orange peel**

In a highball glass, dissolve the sugar in the club soda; then add the ice and liquor. Garnish with fruit peel.

Variations:

Boston Cooler:

Add 1 tablespoon fresh lemon juice, and use light rum.

Floradora Cooler:

Add 1 tablespoon grenadine, and use gin.

Campari Cooler:

Add 1 tablespoon raspberry syrup, and use Campari.

28a–d.

CORDIAL COCKTAILS

General
Description:

The words cordial, apéritif, and liqueur are used inter-changeably. For the purposes of this guidebook, how-ever, the term *cordial cocktails* will designate mixed drinks made with liqueurs. A glance over the variegated colors and curiously shaped bottles of liqueurs in a well-stocked bar may bring to mind an alchemist's workshop. New brands of liqueurs appear every week, making the cordial cocktail the drinker's equivalent of the expanding universe. While prominent liqueur-based cocktails will be found under their own entries, a selection using some popular liqueurs follows.

Purchase:

Look for a bar or restaurant whose liqueur shelves sparkle with the colors of Gothic cathedrals. Since few of us have ever been privy to an alchemist's workshop, a bar specializing in lava lamps will have to do. Cordials are all color and light.

Areas and Time of Occurrence:

☾

Cordials are almost exclusively after-dinner drinks. Served on a patio on a warm night or by a blazing fire in the winter, these exuberant postprandials will crown a memorable meal and mute a mediocre one.

Season:

Ⓜ ☼ ⌘ ❄

A seventeenth-century liqueur maker described his cordial extract as something that "refreshes the spirits and corroborates the brains and other parts of the body." One could safely say that this corroboration would be apropos for any season.

Preparation:

Unlike whiskey or rum, which have very few ingredients, liqueurs are complex little masterpieces that stand on their own, with some containing upward of a hundred flavorings. Because of their subtlety, creativity should be tempered by circumspection when experimenting with cordials.

Flavor Affinities:

By the time you reach for your cordial cocktail, dinner and dessert will be well behind you. Savor it as a "digestif."

Recipes:

Alabama Slammer (Slamma):
1½ ounces amaretto
½ ounce sloe gin
1 ounce Southern Comfort
½ ounce fresh lemon juice

Shake all ingredients with ice; then strain into a chilled cordial glass. Vodka is substituted for amaretto in some versions, and triple sec is also added.

Golden Dream:
1¹/₂ ounces Galliano
¹/₂ ounce fresh orange juice
¹/₂ ounce Cointreau or triple sec
¹/₂ ounce light cream

Shake all ingredients with ice; then strain into a chilled cordial glass.

Horny Leprechaun:
³/₄ ounce Bailey's Irish Cream
³/₄ ounce Rumple Minze
2 dashes of heavy cream

Shake all ingredients with ice; then strain into a chilled cordial glass.

Silent Monk:
1 ounce Bénédictine
¹/₂ ounce Cointreau or triple sec
1 ounce light cream

Shake all ingredients with ice; then strain into a chilled cordial glass.

29a–c. 📷   **COSMOPOLITAN**

General
Description:

The Cosmopolitan is a vodka-based cocktail that has a fruity but tart undertone. In some respects, it is a cousin to the **Margarita**. The Cosmopolitan is a fresh and colorful variant of a **Martini** that needs little getting used to. If the HBO series *Sex and the City* is a reliable indicator of statistics, the Cosmopolitan is the yin to the Martini's yang and is preferred by females.

Unlike many drinks that started out as fads, the Cosmo rapidly ascended into the pantheon of classic cocktails. While several bartenders seem to have experimented with the recipe, no single inventor has laid claim to creating this drink. After Dale DeGroff put it on the Rainbow Room menu in 1996, Madonna was seen drinking one, and DeGroff soon received phone calls from across the globe asking for the recipe. In DeGroff's estimation, the Cosmopolitan is the second-most-recognized cocktail in the world, right after (you guessed it) the Martini.

Purchase:

Since there are a number of twists on the basic recipe, as well as variations, you will need to try numerous cocktail lounges to find the Cosmopolitan that suits you. Once you have found it, ask the bartender what proportions he or she uses. Then, by all means, tell other bartenders your preferences before ordering: more vodka, lime, and so forth. This is also an essential cocktail for the home bartender.

Areas and Time of Occurrence:	You will find the Cosmopolitan in swanky bars and posh nightclubs, at elegant soirées, or on afternoons by the club pool. The Cosmopolitan is also known to go head-to-head and drink-to-drink with the Martini at high-powered business luncheons. Be advised to refrain from ordering a Cosmopolitan at places named Bubba's or Hog Heaven.

Season:	As with all classic cocktails, the Cosmopolitan is a friend to every season. Warmer months are preferable when it is used as an outdoor drink. But with the rising incidence of no-smoking laws, it is not uncommon to see individuals outside a bar on a frigid winter evening, cigarette in one hand and Cosmo in the other. At least it helps the drink keep its chill.

Preparation:	Unlike the Martini, there is very little debate over whether a Cosmopolitan should be shaken or stirred. The consensus is that shaken is the only way to go, so you will need a good cocktail shaker to make this at home. Also, stay away from cranberry juice that is overly adulterated with other juices. Any lemon-flavored (citron) vodka works well for a Cosmopolitan.

The Cosmopolitan is always served neat. The rim of the glass may be rubbed with lime juice and then coated with sugar.

Flavor Affinities:	Cosmos are definitely cocktail hour fare (with the exception of the Cosmopolitan Morning, below).

Because the drink is sweet, salty snacks such as pretzels and nuts or spicy munchies like a Japanese rice cracker mix are all good accompaniments.

Recipes: ***Basic Cosmopolitan:***
2 ounces lemon-infused (citron) vodka
$^1/_2$ ounce Cointreau or triple sec
1 ounce cranberry juice
$^1/_2$ ounce fresh lemon or lime juice
Slice of lemon

 Shake the vodka, Cointreau, cranberry juice, and lime juice with ice; then strain into a chilled cocktail glass. Garnish with a slice of lemon.

Variations: ***Barbados Cosmopolitan:***
Use Mount Gay rum in lieu of vodka.

Cosmopolitan Morning:
Use coffee-flavored vodka in place of lemon-flavored.

Strawberry Cosmopolitan:
2 ounces lemon-infused (citron) vodka
1 ounce cranberry juice
1 ounce strawberry purée, strained of seeds
$^1/_2$ ounce fresh lime juice
Strawberry half

Shake the vodka, cranberry juice, strawberry purée, and lime juice with ice; then strain into a chilled cocktail glass. Garnish with a strawberry half.

Metropolitan:
2 ounces Absolut Kurant vodka
¹/₂ ounce Rose's Lime Juice
1 ounce cranberry juice
¹/₂ ounce fresh lime juice
Slice of lime

Shake the vodka, Rose's Lime Juice, cranberry juice, and fresh lime juice with ice; then strain into a chilled cocktail glass. Garnish with a slice of lime.

Neopolitan:
This lovely variation comes from my alma mater, Boston Bartenders School of America.
2 ounces blackberry-flavored vodka
¹/₂ ounce blue curaçao
¹/₂ ounce cranberry juice
¹/₂ ounce fresh lime juice
Twist of lemon peel

Shake the vodka, blue curaçao, cranberry juice, and lime juice with ice; then strain into a chilled cocktail glass. Garnish with lemon peel.

30a–c.   **"CRAZY COCKTAILS"**

General
Description:

Anything goes in these novelties. There are probably more crazy cocktails than you can stick a shaker at. Along with serious attempts to formulate new classic cocktails, there are others that border on genius and madness—usually the latter. Some may find a permanent place at the bar, but most will go the way of the dodo and the Edsel. A brief Internet search for the phrase "crazy cocktails" yielded some uncanny results. Sparing the reader the likes of the Lobster Lemon Martini and the Avocado Martini, I have included a partial list below (see also **Fishtails**).

Purchase:

Unless you have a mad scientist streak in you, order these cocktails away—far, far away—from home.

Areas and Time
of Occurrence:

If you see a nervous tic in the bartender's eye or a straightjacket hanging on the wall, you have probably discovered the perfect locale for these curiosities.

Season:

Full moons and April Fools' Day seem to be appropriate times to venture down this road of folly.

Preparation:

Revenge may be best served up cold, and so are these cocktails.

Flavor
Affinities:

Uncommon drinks call for uncommon foods, and you may want to sample such international favorites as goat's head soup, prickly pear cactus paddles, or the standby of good old pig's feet.

Recipes: ***Black Lung:***
Also called the "Nicotini," this oddity from the Cathode Ray in Fort Lauderdale, Florida, evidences the old saw "Necessity is the mother of invention." With a nod to strict no-smoking ordinances through-out the country, the Black Lung is made from a blend of a nicotine-infused vodka and Kahlúa.

Garlic Mashed Potato Martini:
Before you shriek, observe the simple ingredients of this "potatoble" served at Lola's in West Hollywood: potato vodka with a garlic clove–stuffed olive.

Peanut Butter Cuptini:
What could possibly be better than a small Reese's Peanut Butter Cup in a Vodka Martini?

World's Most Expensive Cocktail:
Where else but the Trump Tower World Bar in New York would you expect to plunk down $50 for a liba-tion? It's not the Remy XO, Pineau des Charentes, or Veuve Clicquot that supplies the high price, but a floater of 23-karat liquid gold.

31. **CUBA LIBRE (RUM AND COKE)**

General
Description:

The Cuba Libre is a basic white rum drink mixed with Coca-Cola. Those who think that the Cuba Libre is an uninspired drink should take note of its history. Bottled Coca-Cola was barely a decade old during the Spanish-American War when the Rough Riders added Cuban rum to it and loudly toasted "Cuba libre!"— Free Cuba! Some will also recall that Coke's inventor, John Pemberton, used cocaine in the original formula, and one can only imagine what the first Cuba Libre was like. Coke was also only a nickel a bottle, and rum was one of the least expensive of alcohols, so it is no surprise how quickly and extensively the drink caught on. As an aside, H. L. Mencken wrote in his book *The American Language* of a variation: "The troglodytes of western South Carolina coined 'jump stiddy' for a mixture of Coca-Cola and denatured alcohol (usually drawn from automobile radiators); connoisseurs reputedly preferred the taste of what had been aged in Model-T Fords." Stick with the rum.

Purchase:

When you think the bartender will puzzle over which way to hold a cocktail shaker, order this simple drink.

Areas and Time
of Occurrence:

A favorite at afternoon gatherings from pool parties to weddings, the Cuba Libre has come a long way from the campfires of the Rough Riders.

Season: The Cuba Libre almost vanishes during the winter, but as soon as the weather turns warm, it comes mamboing down the highway.

Preparation: Cuban rum should be served in a Cuba Libre, but unless you know someone traveling back from Havana, the chances of finding it are about as remote as winning the lottery. Note that the Cuba Libre goes down easy—too easy. "One too many" does not seem to apply here as much as "four too many." Drinker discretion is advised.

Custom has it that a Cuba Libre may be shaken, but only after it has been drunk—move your feet to the beat of Perez Prado mambo.

Flavor Affinities: Any number of finger foods suit the Cuba Libre. Black bean dip and chips, grilled shrimp skewers, or even Polynesian appetizers are good choices.

Recipe: ***Cuba Libre:***
2 ounces light rum
Cold Coca-Cola
Wedge of lime

 Pour the rum over ice into a chilled highball glass, and add Coke to fill. Squeeze in a lime wedge.

Variation: ***Mexicola:***
Substitute tequila for the rum.

32a–d. 📷 **DAIQUIRI**

General
Description:

The original Daiquiri was a mixture of rum, lime, and sugar, served over ice. Yet another product of late-nineteenth-century imperialism, the Daiquiri was first recorded in a Cuban mining town of the same name. Although the locals had probably been knocking back rum and lime for years, in 1886 an American engineer, James Cox, and a Cuban engineer named Pagliuchi refined the rum and lime drink by adding cane sugar. When Admiral Lucius Johnson introduced the recipe to the Army Navy Club in D.C., in 1909, the Daiquiri was becoming one of the world's most popular drinks. Many years later, John F. Kennedy may have tried his first Daiquiri there. We will never know, but quite ironically, JFK, who also had a penchant for Cuban cigars, designated the Daiquiri as his drink of choice.

Constantino Ribalagua, the famed bartender at Havana's La Floridita—nicknamed La Catedral del Daiquiri—blended the drink with shaved ice, thereby creating the frozen Daiquiri. Chief among the frozen Daiquiri's adherents was Ernest Hemingway. Ribalagua specifically created a sugarless Papa Dobles for Papa Hemingway, who apparently could wade through a dozen of these at one sitting. Standing is not an option after a dozen frozen Daiquiris.

Purchase:

Bars are continually experimenting with this versatile cocktail. Fruit may be used, and the drink may be mixed with ice in a blender, but it should always be made fresh. This essential cocktail should be in the repertoire of every home bartender.

Areas and Time
of Occurrence:
☀ ☾

A classic, shaken Daiquiri served while you watch the tall ships come in is a thing of beauty. A machine-produced frozen Daiquiri at all-you-can-drink night at the local chain cocktail lounge is a travesty. Odious Daiquiris are everywhere, so watch where you step.

Season:
☀

Breathe in the salt sea air, feel the cool evening breeze as it dissipates the summer heat, and by all means order a frosty Daiquiri.

Preparation:

Supposedly Ribalagua gently squeezed the lime with his fingers to avoid getting any bitter oil from the peel in the drink. After shaking the icy cocktail, he strained it through a fine sieve. Following this exact procedure for every drink would have been incredibly time-consuming after Hemingway popularized it, but it does demonstrate that a proper Daiquiri is a studied balance in harmony. An excess of lime will make the drink bitter, while too much rum is overpowering. It should also be shaken to the point of frothiness.

Flavor
Affinities:

The Daiquiri is affable and open to suggestions. Here are but a few: crudités with red caviar dip, Chinese duck parcels wrapped in rice paper, and assorted melon chunk skewers with Spanish ham.

Recipes:

Classic Daiquiri:
1 1/2 ounces light rum
1 ounce fresh lime juice
1 teaspoon simple syrup or superfine sugar

Shake all ingredients very well with ice; then strain into a chilled cocktail glass.

Hemingway Daiquiri (Papa Dobles):
Juice of 2 limes
Juice of 1 grapefruit
2 ounces light rum
1/4 ounce maraschino liqueur

Mix all ingredients over cracked or shaved ice; then pour into a chilled highball glass.

Classic Frozen Daiquiri:
3 ounces light rum
1 1/2 ounces fresh lime juice
1 teaspoon simple syrup or superfine sugar

Combine all ingredients in a blender with 1/2 cup cracked ice. Blend until frothy, and serve in a large cocktail glass.

Variations:

Frozen Banana Daiquiri:
Add a sliced banana before blending.

Frozen Strawberry Daiquiri:
Add 1/2 cup fresh strawberries before blending.

DAISIES

General
Description:

*A medium-tall drink, the daisy is a fruit juice–based
cocktail that is sweetened with grenadine or a red
liqueur.* Yet another "old-timer" that has more than a
century under its belt, daisies are a sumptuous relative
of cobblers and fixes. A daisy always has a red tinge to
it and is occasionally finished by a compatible liqueur
floated on top at the last second. The name Daisy
seemingly derives not from the flower but from slang
for something extraordinary—from which the word
doozy is also derived.

Purchase:

If cobblers and fixes are becoming rare, daisies are all
but gone. Make this drink at home for an adventurous group of friends.

Areas and Time
of Occurrence:

Unless you make daisies at home, you will need a
first-class ticket to the Twilight Zone to find them.

Season:

Plan an outdoor summer cocktail party and feature a
variety of daisies. Put on some Glenn Miller or Benny
Goodman, and imagine yourself in another world.

Preparation:

To separate them from other drinks, daisies were

often served in elaborate, heavy glassware or silver mugs. The latter also keeps the drink cool.

Flavor
Affinities:

Daisies can be a little sweet for some tastes, so try matching them with savory or hearty foods like smoked turkey or cheddar and onion canapés.

Recipe:

Gin Daisy:
2 ounces gin
¹/₂ ounce fresh lemon juice
2 teaspoons grenadine
Cold club soda
Slice of lemon and sprig of mint

Shake the gin, lemon juice, and grenadine with ice; then strain into a chilled glass filled with cracked ice. Add club soda to fill. Garnish with a lemon slice and a mint sprig.

Variation:

Bourbon Daisy:
Substitute bourbon for the gin, and float 2 teaspoons Southern Comfort on top just before serving.

34a–b.

DUBONNET COCKTAIL (ZAZA)

General
Description:

There is no substitute for Dubonnet in this cocktail. Mixed with gin, this drink is finished with a twist of lemon. As simple as the Dubonnet Cocktail would appear to be, as with the **Martini**, a debate exists over what the proportions should be and what else should go in it. The cocktail was popularized by an ad campaign in the 1960s, but its basic ingredients made it a Prohibition standard before that. Created in the 1850s, red Dubonnet is a wine-based spirit that included quinine to help the French troops in North Africa fight off malaria. You may have little chance of contracting yellow fever, but this drink is a sure way to cure the blues.

Purchase:

When you find the **Cosmopolitan** a little too sweet or the Martini too dry, try a Dubonnet Cocktail for a crisp change of pace.

Areas and Time of Occurrence:

The Dubonnet Cocktail epitomizes the chic, sleek drink to be sipped in casual elegance. Cocktail hour in a classic wood-paneled bar is where the Dubonnet Cocktail is best appreciated.

Season:

Dubonnet is drunk as an apéritif all year long in France, and the same could be proposed for the Dubonnet Cocktail.

Preparation:

The earliest recipes for the Dubonnet Cocktail call for equal parts Dubonnet and gin; while tastes may vary, the original still seems the way to go. A point of contention is whether to use bitters. New York bartender Gary Regan resolves this issue beautifully by adding a flamed orange peel (page 21) to the drink.

Flavor Affinities:	Skip the beer nuts here; the Dubonnet Cocktail should be accompanied by memorable appetizers. Pâté de foie gras, endive boats with smoked salmon, or deviled eggs with capers would all do nicely.

Recipe:
Dubonnet Cocktail:
1¹/₂ ounces gin
1¹/₂ ounces red Dubonnet
Dash of bitters (optional)
Twist of lemon peel

Shake the gin, Dubonnet, and bitters with ice, and strain into a chilled cocktail glass. Garnish with lemon peel.

Variation:
Lady Madonna:
Substitute red vermouth for the gin.

35a–b.

FISHTAILS

General Description:
As the name implies, these unique cocktails are actually made with fish. Octopus in the Water, the Uni Shooter, and the Baby Octopus Saketini are among the new-school varieties of seafood cocktails with clout. Oysters, smoked and fresh, seem to be the critters of choice. Shrimp, clams, bits of shellfish, and sea

urchins are all also floating about in cocktails these days, though the Japanese have been wading through these drinks for ages.

Chef Daisuke Utagawa of Sushi-Ko in Washington, D.C., refined the oyster Martini by replacing the oyster with uni, a tiny sea urchin, giving the world the Uni Shooter. Gary and Mardee Regan reproduce the recipe in *New Classic Cocktails*. It was accidentally created when Utagawa made the mistake of asking for uni instead of oyster. You decide what kind of mistake it was. Nevertheless, judging by the number of restaurants that feature variations on their menus, these curious drinks are appealing to seafood lovers from coast to coast. Fishtails are proof that you can have your crab cake and drink it too.

Purchase: Sushi bars are the laboratories for these cocktails.

Areas and Time   Nearly any restaurant that serves the freshest fish and
of Occurrence: sushi will be game to experiment with these cocktails.
     Whether your date will be is another matter entirely. If you are both up to the challenge, be bold and order them right up front. Otherwise, you may need to imbibe some more conventional fortification first.

Season: Oysters are at their peak in the cooler months, so
     order drinks with that bivalve during those months. Order a fishtail any time of the year you have a craving for an octopus or the like in your cocktail.

Preparation: Most fishtails are just variations on traditional cocktails, and little additional preparation knowledge is
required. If, however, you opt for fugu fins in your
cocktail, be aware that these blowfish fins are poison-
ous and will kill you if not prepared properly. You will
need to hire a professional fugu chef for this. When
not using smoked or precooked fish, always buy fresh,
sushi-grade seafood. Some recipes call for soy, but
ponzu sauce—a soy-vinegar dipping sauce often
served with gyoza—cuts the fishiness of the drink.

Flavor
Affinities: You might immediately think sushi would pair well
with these cocktails, but don't jump into the ocean
too early. Begin with gyoza, crispy noodles, or a
mixed salad.

Recipes: **_The Unitini:_**
2 ounces chilled sake
1 small piece uni (sea urchin)
1 raw quail egg yolk
1 dab of wasabi
4 dashes of ponzu sauce
Cucumber stick
Several small, thin strips of nori (dried seaweed)

 Pour the sake into a chilled cocktail glass; then add
the uni, quail egg, and wasabi. Dribble the ponzu
sauce along the rim of the glass, slide in the cucumber
stick, and then garnish with the nori.

Variations:

Clamitini:

Substitute 1 littleneck clam for the uni, and scallion for the cucumber.

Baby Octopus Sakétini:

TenPenh in Washington, D.C., serves this typical vodka and sake Martini with a pickled baby octopus. Wouldn't you?

Oyster Martini:
3 ounces vodka
¹/₂ ounce dry vermouth
1 smoked oyster

Shake the vodka and vermouth with ice; then strain into a chilled cocktail glass. Drop in the oyster. Alternatively, use a fresh oyster in season.

Oyster Shooter:
Dash of red Tabasco
Dash of green Tabasco
Dash of cocktail sauce
Dash of horseradish
1 ounce vodka
1 fresh, cold oyster
Wedge of lemon

Shake the Tabascos, cocktail sauce, horseradish, and vodka with ice; then strain into a large shot glass.

Drop in the oyster, bite the lemon, and down the drink. Say goodnight, Gracie.

36a–b.

FLIP

General Description:

In an "iron flip dog," eggs, sugar, cream, spices, molasses, and even pumpkin are scalded in a mug using a hot fireplace poker. Any number of alcohols are then added. Few mixed drinks have the lineage of a flip. It was first mentioned in England in 1685, and Ishmael expounds upon its virtues in *Moby Dick*. When eggs were added, the flip was called a "Yard of Flannel," alluding to the flannel-like surface caused by the cooked eggs. The heated flip has all but vanished, and the drink has literally taken a polar flip, since it is now served as a chilled cocktail. The iron pokers were also known as loggerheads; the expression "at loggerheads," used for being in a heated dispute, derives from the heated discussions born of a surfeit of flips.

Purchase:

Hot pokers are not common bar tools anymore, so a true flip would be best sampled at home.

Areas and Time of Occurrence:

One would be wise to avoid tippling a flip aboard a ship, since the drink will be much diluted and pickled by the salt spray, according to Ishmael. Flips are not necessarily dry, but the places to drink them should be.

Season:	The traditional, heated flip is a cool-weather drink that can be enjoyed in front of a holiday fire or as an excellent après-ski invigorator. Cold flips may be enjoyed anytime.
Preparation:	A flip should be frothy; it is therefore important to shake it vigorously.
Flavor Affinities:	After a day on the slopes, arrange a fondue party. Swedish meatballs would also go well here.
Recipe:	***Flip:*** **1¹⁄₂ ounces desired liquor (brandy, sherry, port, and so forth)** **1 small egg** **1 teaspoon superfine sugar** **¹⁄₂ ounce heavy cream (optional)** **Freshly ground nutmeg**
	Shake the liquor, egg, sugar, and cream very well with ice to emulsify the egg; then strain into a sour or wine glass. Dust with nutmeg.
Variation:	***Hot Brandy Flip:*** Beat brandy, egg, and sugar in a mug. Fill with hot milk, and garnish with nutmeg.

37a–b. **FRAPPÉ**

General Description:

A frappé is a combination of almost any kind of liqueurs served over crushed or shaved ice. As its name implies, a frappé is a dessert drink. It also makes an ideal finale to a meal in lieu of the usual ice cream or cake. To make a perfect frappé, you must think outside the box of cookies. The skillful balance of liqueurs provides a dessert in and of itself. If you are watching some calories but not all of them, the frappé may be the start of your new diet regimen.

Purchase:

Frappés are best suited to the conviviality of hearth and home. Serve them to good friends.

Areas and Time of Occurrence:

You know that your date or guests will probably want a postprandial as well as something sweet after their meal. A frappé will fittingly satisfy all their cravings.

Season:

Like dessert, a frappé may be served at any time.

Preparation:

Frappé glasses, also known as parfait glasses, are available, but you may also use a deep-saucer champagne glass. You may mix frappés fresh, but Thomas Mario, in his *Playboy's Host and Bar Book*, suggests swizzling them and placing them in the freezer beforehand.

Flavor Affinities:

If you must serve food, serve fruit that matches the liqueurs in the frappé.

Recipe:

All-White Frappé:
$^1/_2$ ounce anisette
$^1/_4$ ounce white crème de menthe
$^1/_2$ ounce white crème de cacao
1 teaspoon fresh lemon juice

Stir all ingredients without ice. Pour over crushed or shaved ice in a deep-saucer champagne glass.

Variations:

Mixed Mocha Frappé:
Substitute $^3/_4$ ounce coffee liqueur for the anisette, and $^1/_4$ ounce triple sec for the lemon juice.

Banana Rum Frappé:
Use $^1/_2$ ounce each banana liqueur, light rum, and fresh orange juice.

38a–c.

FROZEN DRINKS

General
Description:

When blended properly, any number of frozen drinks can be made from a diversity of spirits. The frozen drink is proof that good and evil dwell in the world. Lip-tingling frozen **Daiquiris** and **Margaritas** were concocted to provide cooling relief on sultry days—and then came the marketing pundits and pub chains to obliterate their work. Slushy, sickeningly sweet Margaritas are pumped out of bar hoses, and one Daiquiri chain concocts such travesties as the Bubble

Gum, the Dreamsicle, and the Triple Bypass. Our advice: Bypass these aberrations. Fortunately, there are still many bartenders dedicated to offsetting this ignoble trend. Classic frozen drinks will be found under their main entries, but the recipes here can serve as a basis for other permutations.

Purchase: Look around a bar that seems to be serving many frozen drinks. If you don't see a blender or hear that familiar whir, the drinks are probably prepackaged, and it's time to move on to another bar, or city. Alternatively, experiment with frozen drinks at home, where at least you will know what you're getting.

Areas and Time of Occurrence: Daytime or nighttime, you will find frozen drinks seaside, poolside, and curbside in resort towns. Ask the locals who makes the best; steer clear of any cocktail dispensers that look like they could put gasoline in a Hummer. Since most ingredients can be premeasured, these cocktails are easily adaptable to making large batches to be served up for thirsty friends.

Season: Summer is a given for the enjoyment of frozen drinks. If you are also partial to cold showers and swims with the Polar Bear Club, winter will do just as well.

Preparation: Frozen drinks should always be made fresh with the best ingredients and properly crushed ice. You will need a very good blender here.

Flavor
Affinities:

Spicy foods and hot hors d'oeuvres will further bring out the chill of frozen drinks. Crunchy tempura vegetable skewers or deep-fried wontons with hot chili dipping sauce are just a couple of possibilities.

Recipes:

Blue Berkeley:
1½ ounces light rum
½ ounce brandy
1 tablespoon passion fruit syrup
1 tablespoon fresh lemon juice
Pineapple round

Combine the rum, brandy, passion fruit syrup, and lemon juice in a blender with ⅓ cup crushed ice, and pulse until smooth. Pour into a champagne flute, and garnish with a pineapple round fitted over the rim.

Smooth Operator:
1½ ounces Frangelico
½ ounce Kahlúa
½ ounce Bailey's Irish Cream
½ banana
4 ounces heavy cream
Pineapple slice

Combine the Frangelico, Kahlúa, Bailey's Irish Cream, banana, and cream in a blender with ⅓ cup crushed ice, and puree briefly until smooth. Pour into a margarita or wine glass, and garnish with pineapple.

Frozen Apple:
1¹/₂ ounces applejack or apple brandy
¹/₂ ounce fresh lime juice
1 teaspoon superfine sugar or simple syrup

Put all ingredients in a blender with ¹/₃ cup crushed ice, and blend. Pour into a chilled champagne goblet.

FUZZY NAVEL

General Description:

A latecomer to the dubious pantheon of liqueurs, peach schnapps is blended with orange juice to create the Fuzzy Navel. No one has laid claim to originating the Fuzzy Navel, which, considering its many detractors, is a darned good thing. It was one of the first of the 1980s new wave of mixed drinks, a craze for drinks lambasted by *New York Times* critic William Grimes as "a kind of cult, rallying points for young drinkers in search of fun and not too picky about taste." The *fuzzy* in the drink name references the peach, and the *navel* refers to the orange. The drink spawned such other cutesy innuendos as the Woo Woo. One suspects that after too many of those you would need to repair to the tinkle-dinkle-ha-ha room for relief.

Purchase:

The Fuzzy Navel and its progeny are usually such simple drinks that even the most unaccomplished bartenders could whip them up in their sleep—and usually do.

Areas and Time of Occurrence:	As a rule, bars named after people will probably not serve the Fuzzy Navel. However, lounges named for exotic birds, articles of intimate apparel, and small reptiles will. And just like the woodland creatures that only come out at night, that is also when you will find the Fuzzy Navel in all its peachy glory.
Season:	The Fuzzy Navel is in demand throughout the year.
Preparation:	If simplicity is your game, you will score well with the Fuzzy Navel. These sneaky little devils also creep up on the drinker, giving *fuzzy* a further connotation. Using grapefruit juice will produce a Fuzzy Pucker. Don't go there.
Flavor Affinities:	The Fuzzy Navel could very well become the new brunch drink. Since it probably won't, however, stick with mixed nuts.
Recipe:	***Fuzzy Navel:*** **2 ounces peach schnapps** **6 ounces fresh orange juice** **Fruit of choice**

Pour the schnapps and orange juice over ice in a chilled highball glass. Garnish with your fruit of choice.

Variation:	***Woo Woo:*** Substitute cranberry juice for the orange juice.

40. **GIMLET**

General
Description:

Originally a gin-based drink with lime juice, the Gimlet has gained much more favor with the vodka crowd. Philip Marlowe in Raymond Chandler's *The Long Goodbye* is instructed that a Gimlet could only be made with Rose's lime juice. Although bartenders almost unanimously use Rose's, the original gin Gimlet is vying with vodka to such a degree that you would be advised to specify which spirit you want. According to the *Dictionary of Eponyms*, British Navy doctor T. O. Gimlette prescribed the drink as a medicinal tonic and as a dilution to gin, which he believed clouded the minds of the recruits when sipped neat.

Purchase:

Not all bars keep fresh fruit on hand, and the Gimlet is a handy alternative to a **Gin and Tonic** as a serviceable scurvy preventative.

Areas and Time
of Occurrence:

The proverbial "old-man's bar" is the befitting crusty venue for a Gimlet. The sun must be down, and it helps if someone named Big Al is asleep on the bar top with his head in the pretzel basket.

Season:

The driest days of summer call out for the cooling tartness of a Gimlet.

Preparation:

Whether you serve your Gimlet neat or over ice, always shake the ingredients with plenty of ice first.

Do not substitute fresh lime juice for preserved lime juice. Doing so, with the addition of sugar, will produce a **Gin Rickey**.

Flavor
Affinities:

The lime wedge served with your Gimlet might be the only food available in the bar. Given a choice, smoked oysters and bacon-wrapped chicken livers are blasts from the past that pair nicely with this drink. Stay away from the basket of pretzels and Big Al.

Recipe:

Gimlet:
2 ounces gin (or vodka)
¼ ounce Rose's Lime Juice
Wedge of lime

Shake the gin and lime juice with ice; then strain into a chilled cocktail glass or into an old-fashioned glass full of ice. Garnish with a lime wedge.

41. **GIN AND TONIC**

General
Description:

Gin and the quinine-derived tonic may be at the heart of a Gin and Tonic, but there is much more in its soul. In his book *On Drink*, Kingsley Amis quips, "It would be rather shabby to take money for explaining that, for instance, a gin and tonic consists of gin and tonic, plus ice and a slice of lemon." Money matters aside, the lack of preparation details in most cocktail books takes the Gin and Tonic—or other tonic drinks—for granted. But who among us has not had an appalling G&T? A good Gin and Tonic, Gin Tonic, or Gin Tonny must be cold and not overwhelmed by tonic, as is the case in most printed recipes.

Historically, quinine has been taken as an antidote to fevers for hundreds of years. In seventeenth-century India, the British mixed it with gin and lemon juice to reduce the quinine's bitterness. Schweppes, a company that perfected carbonated mineral water in the 1780s, introduced their tonic water in the 1870s. It soon became popular with British troops as a premixed, curiously refreshing alternative. The fact that Amis and much of the world prefer lemon to lime is another issue entirely.

Purchase:

Sadly, most bars gush gallons of tonic from a multi-beverage hose, and residue of cola or ginger ale can linger. Look for a bar that still serves individual bottles of tonic with each drink.

Areas and Time of Occurrence:

The G&T is a common convivial bar staple, but it is also a comforting companion to the individual seeking solace from the journey through yet another exhausting day. Whether you have spent an afternoon averting computer viruses or going for that final point in a competitive tennis match, the Gin and Tonic revives, stimulates, and helps to unwind.

Season:

A Gin and Tonic is welcome in any season, but sitting with a book on your lap and this drink by your side on an early summer evening may redefine civilization.

Preparation:

As distinctive as every brand of gin can be, so, too, is the Gin and Tonic. Many agree that it is a waste of money to use imported gin when a domestic will do just fine, so let budget and taste be your guide. But never skimp on the tonic! Unless you are hosting a party, only use 10-ounce bottles. Few abominations compare with flat tonic. European Schweppes, which has more of a quinine taste to it, makes a superior G&T, but good luck finding it elsewhere in the world. Bubbly effervescence is paramount, and one or two gentle stirs is enough to blend the flavors.

Flavor Affinities:

The G&T is a no-nonsense drink that deserves humble but assertive foods. Little more is required than extra-sharp cheddar wedges on crackers, accompanied by cubes of ham.

Recipe:

Classic Gin and Tonic:
3 ounces gin
Tonic
Wedge of lime (or lemon)

Fill a chilled old-fashioned glass halfway with ice cubes, and pour in the gin. Gently rub the lime wedge around the rim of the glass, squeeze in a few drops of juice, and drop the lime into the glass. Top with tonic, and gently stir once or twice.

Variations:

Vodka and Tonic:
Substitute vodka for the gin.

Rum and Tonic:
Substitute light rum for the gin.

 42a–c.

GIN COCKTAILS

General
Description:

Any number of combinations make up a gin cocktail—as long as it also has gin. Gin has gone through many manifestations since its creation in the seventeenth century, and the subsequent cocktails using gin exemplify the changing flavors and tastes. Easily produced, albeit in its crudest form, gin was inexpensive to make as well as to purchase. This made it a boon during Prohibition. That it tasted like something used to dress wounds fostered an age of drinks created by speakeasy bartenders to mask the astringent taste. In this respect, the "Noble Experiment," as Prohibition was called, actually contributed significantly to the diversity of the gin cocktail. Gin and Italian vermouth—shortened to "Gin and It"—became one of the most popular creations. The more common gin drinks are listed in their own entries, but some intriguing old and new options are presented here.

Purchase:	Traditional bars will be happy to dig into the past and mix some bygone cocktails; hot spots are always stirring up novel concoctions.
Areas and Time of Occurrence:	From the dark backrooms of Prohibition speakeasies to the magnolia-shaded verandas of Kentucky, or from the back alleys to the bar rail at the Savoy, gin has easily made its home wherever it has hung—and often forgotten—its hat.
Season:	The myriad classic gin drinks and the ensuing newcomers defy pigeonholing.
Flavor Affinities:	Casual or elegant high-protein foods, from riblets to sirloin tips, are preferable to starchy foods.

Recipes:

Gin and It:
2 ounces gin
1 ounce sweet vermouth
Dash of bitters
Twist of orange peel

Stir the gin, vermouth, and bitters in a cocktail glass, and garnish with orange peel. This is generally served without ice, but you may want to use ice-cold gin.

Variations:

Gin and French:
Substitute French vermouth for the sweet vermouth.

Gin and Sin:
1 ounce gin
1 ounce fresh lemon juice
1 tablespoon fresh orange juice
Dash of grenadine

Shake all ingredients with ice; then strain into a chilled cocktail glass.

Gin Southern:
1¹/₂ ounces gin
¹/₂ ounce Southern Comfort
¹/₄ ounce fresh grapefruit juice
¹/₄ ounce fresh lemon juice
Sprig of mint

Shake the gin, Southern Comfort, grapefruit juice, and lemon juice with ice; then strain into a chilled cocktail glass. Garnish with a mint sprig.

Pink Gin (Gin and Bitters):
2 ounces gin
3 dashes of bitters
Twist of lemon peel

Stir the gin and bitters in a cocktail glass, and garnish with lemon peel. This is generally served without ice, but you may want to chill the gin in the freezer. The British occasionally add water or a splash of soda.

43a–c. 📷   **GIN FIZZ**

General
Description:

Fizzes are any number of sour-based cocktails with the mandatory addition of club soda and lemon juice. Gin was the earliest spirit used in a fizz. The Gin Fizz, which is a close relation to the **Tom Collins**, has been satisfying bar patrons for more than a hundred years. One of the defining differences between a Gin Fizz and a Tom Collins is the glass size. Highball glasses containing 8 to 12 ounces are preferred for a fizz, while the larger collins glass is, not surprisingly, preferred for a collins. The Ramos Gin Fizz, formulated by the Ramos brothers in New Orleans in the late 1880s, remains popular today, especially as a hangover cure. Legend has it that the initial Ramos Gin Fizz required so much vigorous shaking that it was passed among patrons until their arms tired. Right.

Purchase:

As basic as a Gin Fizz or Sloe Gin Fizz may be, all bartenders seem to have their own signature on this cocktail. Try it at home for a little forgery of your own.

Areas and Time
of Occurrence:
☀

The Gin Fizz is a light, refreshing cocktail to sip in the club after a golf game or in an airport lounge for a little courage before a short flight. The Ramos Gin Fizz is almost exclusively a morning-after libation.

Season:
🌱☀🍂❄

Not bone-chillingly cold, the Gin Fizz is well adapted to all seasons. But the sparkling club soda over ice makes a fizz a classic summer drink.

Preparation: You will need a sturdy shaker for any fizz that includes
egg whites. The Ramos Gin Fizz calls for orange
flower water, which may be found in specialty food
stores. You can use mineral water in place of club soda,
but select one that is neutral in flavor. Fizzes are rarely
garnished, and parsimoniously so when they are.

Flavor
Affinities: For warm appetizers, try caramelized onion tartlets,
curried vegetable filo packets, or marinated button
mushrooms with crusty bread at room temperature.

Recipes: *Gin Fizz:*
2 ounces gin
3/4 ounce fresh lemon juice
1 teaspoon superfine sugar or simple syrup
Cold club soda
Sprig of mint

Shake the gin, lemon juice, and sugar with ice; then
strain into a 10-ounce highball glass filled with ice.
Add club soda to fill, and garnish with a mint sprig.

Ramos Gin Fizz:
2 ounces gin
1/2 ounce fresh lemon juice
1/2 ounce fresh lime juice
1 egg white

1 ounce heavy cream
2 teaspoons superfine sugar
1/2 teaspoon orange flower water
Cold club soda

Vigorously shake the gin, lemon juice, lime juice, egg white, cream, sugar, and orange flower water with ice; then strain into a 10-ounce highball glass without ice. Pour in club soda to fill.

Sloe Gin Fizz:
1 ounce sloe gin
1 ounce gin
3/4 ounce fresh lemon juice
Cold club soda
Slice of lemon

Shake the sloe gin, gin, and lemon juice with ice; then strain into a highball glass filled with ice. Add club soda to fill, and garnish with a lemon slice.

44a–b. **GIN RICKEY**

General
Description:

The Gin Rickey was the first in a long line of Rickeys— long dry cocktails over ice, usually made without sweeteners. Washington, D.C., is known for its movers, mixers, and shakers, but rarely are drinks named for them. Lobbyists are known to kick back a few with members of Congress, and Joe Rickey was no exception. After Rickey ordered seconds of a new gin drink at Shoemaker's Restaurant, the bartender named the cocktail the Gin Rickey. It may not be so coincidental, then, that Rickey became the first major U.S. importer of limes.

Purchase:

The Gin Rickey may be an old-school cocktail, but its simplicity has opened the way to many present-day variations.

Areas and Time of Occurrence:

The Rickey soon evolved from a gin drink to one that substituted any number of various spirits. Those who enjoy the finesse of a **Cosmopolitan** but are looking for a taller alternative may want to experiment with a Rickey at their after-hours gatherings.

Season:

The Gin Rickey is a classic warm-weather cooler, but it is also ideal for long hours on the dance floor when you want a thirst quencher that won't send you under the table.

Preparation:

You never need to shake a Rickey. Merely pour your ingredients into the glass. If you substitute ginger ale for club soda, the cocktail becomes a Buck.

Flavor Affinities:

With the Gin Rickey's origins resting in the politicians' lair, one might immediately think of pairing it with hot tongue and bologna sandwiches. The latter-

day visitations of Rickeys are so diverse that foods
from sushi to tandoori-style chicken bites all fare well.

Recipe: ***Gin Rickey:***
1¹/₂ ounces gin
¹/₂ ounce fresh lime juice
Cold club soda
Wedge of lime

Pour the gin and lime juice over ice in a chilled highball glass. Add club soda to fill. Gently rub the lime
wedge around the rim of the glass, squeeze in a few
drops of juice, and drop the lime into the glass.

Variations: ***Twister:***
Substitute vodka for the gin, and lemon soda for the
club soda.

Tequila Rickey:
Rim the glass with lime and salt first; then substitute
tequila for the gin.

Cosmo Rickey:
1¹/₂ ounces lemon-infused (citron) vodka
¹/₂ ounce Cointreau or triple sec
Splash of cranberry juice
¹/₂ ounce fresh lime juice
Cold club soda
Slice each of lime and orange

Pour the vodka, Cointreau, cranberry juice, and lime juice over ice in a chilled highball glass. Add club soda to fill. Garnish with slices of lime and orange.

45a–b. **GIRL SCOUT COOKIE**

General Description:

The Girl Scout Cookie is one of the numerous liquid confections that attempt to simulate a favorite foodstuff. When the **Black Russian** entered the bar scene, some stalwart traditionalists protested, "They've gone about as far as they can go!" The Girl Scout Cookie and the dozens of other cookie, cake, and candy variants would have them spinning in their graves. The Girl Scout Cookie affirms that there is a new generation of bar-hopping adventurers who want to have it their way. If only Troop 42 could get a cut of the bar profits!

Purchase:

Lounges of the swinging, under-thirties crowd were the proving grounds for the Girl Scout Cookie drink, but college dorms are rapidly becoming the Willie Wonka world of sweet-tooth sorcery.

Areas and Time of Occurrence:

Campy chic? Women at the bar tying cherry stems with their tongues? Music ranging from Sinatra to the New York Dolls? All in the same place? There is a very good chance you will have no problem ordering a Girl Scout Cookie here.

Season:	Impetuosity and partying in the first degree are the only seasonal requirements for these confections.
Preparation:	Shake, strain, pour, and boogie.
Flavor Affinities:	One would imagine that these wildly sweet drinks would require no accompaniment, but after too many of them, a **Bloody Mary** is advisable the next morning.
Recipe:	***Girl Scout Cookie:*** **³/₄ ounce peppermint schnapps** **³/₄ ounce dark crème de cacao** **¹/₂ ounce heavy cream**
	Shake all ingredients with ice; then strain into an old-fashioned or highball glass filled with ice.
Variations:	***Almond Joy:*** Substitute amaretto for the peppermint schnapps.
	Chocolate Cake: Substitute ¹/₂ ounce each of Frangelico and vodka for the peppermint schnapps and crème de cacao.

GODFATHER

General Description:	*The Godfather is one of numerous cocktails named for notable films.* Given the popularity of the Godfather

46a–c.

films, few would question the source of this cocktail's name. The practice of naming cocktails after popular films, plays, or other entertainments has long been an established tradition. The Matrix and the Reservoir Dog are now less known than the Adonis, but the Godfather is still doing favors for those who order it. We may also wonder why there were no drinks named after *High Noon* or *Lost Weekend*. For cocktails named after celebrities, see the **Mary Pickford**.

Purchase:

Most cinema cocktails are as fleeting as their namesakes' runs on the silver screen. Film buffs may want to peruse the contents of their home bar and begin directing epics of their own.

Areas and Time of Occurrence:

Look for bars or lounges with a Hollywood or cinematic theme. Is there a Bar Noir in your town? If not, you may have another job opportunity in your future.

Season:

Whether it's springtime in the Alps, endless summer, Cheyenne autumn, or winter vacation, the Godfather is a man for all seasons.

Preparation:

Unlike the films for which they were named, the Godfather and other cinema cocktails are fairly straightforward.

Flavor Affinities:

For a Godfather, I would recommend the veal. . . .

Recipes: **Godfather:**
              2 ounces Scotch
              1 ounce amaretto

 Pour both ingredients over ice in a chilled old-fashioned glass, and stir.

The Matrix:
2 ounces tequila
1 ounce fresh orange juice
1/2 ounce crème de cassis
1/2 ounce caramel liqueur

 Shake all ingredients with ice; then strain into a chilled cocktail glass.

Reservoir Dog:
2 ounces Jägermeister
2 ounces Bailey's Irish Cream

 Shake both ingredients with ice; then strain into a chilled cocktail glass.

Gone with the Wind (aka Scarlett O'Hara):
2 ounces Southern Comfort
Cranberry juice
Wedge of lime

 Pour the Southern Comfort over ice in a chilled highball glass. Add cranberry juice to fill, and squeeze in a lime wedge.

GROG

47a–b.

General Description:

In its earliest incarnation, grog was merely a mixture of hot rum and water with an occasional sprinkling of spices. The eighteenth-century British admiral Edward Vernon, nicknamed Old Grog for the grogram fabric cloak he wore, attempted to prevent scurvy among his men by serving them a pint of rum a day. The dark navy rum had nothing to do with scurvy, but it did have a way of knocking them on their duffle bags. Vernon then issued the infamous Captain's Order Number 349, stating that all rum should be mixed with water, a dash of brown sugar, and lime to make it more palatable. In their displeasure, the sailors christened the weakened beverage after the admiral.

Grog has undergone many refinements over the years and is now served comfortingly warm or refreshingly cool. The original rum used in grog did not become available to the public until the 1980s. That it made its way to the liquor store shelves was more than coincidental or generous on the part of the manufacturer—the British Navy phased out the daily ration of rum in the late 1970s. The rum is now sold under the label Pusser's Navy Rum—*pusser* being slang for the *purser* who distributed it. The phrase *grog blossoms* is a reference to the broken blood vessels in the nose caused by drinking too much.

Purchase:

Large bars and cocktail lounges tend to favor the cooler, more elaborate recipes for grog. That should be an incentive for mixing this drink at home.

Areas and Time of Occurrence:

Since grog is drunk hot or cold, it keeps unusual hours and finds itself in disparate venues. A traditional mug of warm grog is just as welcome during halftime at a football game as it is after a day of skiing, but a chilled cup of grog at sunset by the shore is equally appealing.

Season:

In its earliest years, grog, like most spirits, was drunk warm throughout the year. With the coming of the "ice age" of mixed drinks in the late 1800s, warm grog was relegated to strictly a cool-weather potable.

Preparation:

For warm grog, dark rum is preferable. Molasses was an early sweetener, but honey has supplanted it. Use a light rum or a blend of rums in a cold grog.

Flavor Affinities:

Try a full fondue spread with cheese, meat, and vegetables for warm grog; set out a medley of dips and chips for its cool cousin.

Recipes:

Traditional Grog:
2 ounces dark rum

½ ounce fresh lime juice
1 teaspoon brown sugar
4 ounces hot water
Slice of orange and a cinnamon stick

Mix the rum, lime juice, brown sugar, and hot water in a mug. Garnish with an orange slice and a cinnamon stick.

Grog Cocktail (Navy Grog):
1 ounce light rum
1 ounce dark rum
1 ounce 151-proof rum
2 ounces fresh orange juice
1 ounce unsweetened pineapple juice
Slice of orange and a maraschino cherry

Shake the three rums and the two juices with ice; then strain into a chilled old-fashioned glass filled with ice. Garnish with an orange slice and a maraschino cherry.

48a–b.

HARVEY WALLBANGER

General
Description:

Vodka makes up the lion's share of a Harvey Wallbanger, but it's the dash of Galliano that makes it distinct. People may remember the name of this very 1970s cocktail, but few, if any, still order it. One of numerous stories has it that the drink was mixed for a disconsolate surfer named Harvey, who downed several Screwdrivers laced with Galliano and then summarily banged into walls while exiting the bar. More likely, it was Galliano liqueur's enormous advertising campaign featuring a goofy cartoon character called Harvey that made the Harvey Wallbanger one of the hippest drinks of the 1970s. Its success followed on the heels of the **Moscow Mule**, but the Wallbanger has similarly joined the "endangered species list" and been put out to pasture with the Mule.

Purchase:

If the bartender thinks you are speaking in tongues when you ask for a Harvey Wallbanger, order a Screwdriver with a splash of Galliano on top and hope the bartender remembers for next time.

Areas and Time of Occurrence:

The Harvey Wallbanger was meant to appeal to the surfing, tie-dyed shirt and sandals set. Beaches, pools, tiki lounges, and wherever anyone might sit sipping out of a coconut without attracting a second glance are all acceptable places to order one.

Season:

As the legend behind this drink would imply, the Harvey Wallbanger is a summertime drink. Remembering exactly what season it is after banging into walls is your own business.

Preparation:

Copying the simplicity of a Moscow Mule, the Wallbanger created a special mug in which to serve the drink. And as if the drink weren't simple enough, there is a picture of Harvey on the mug holding a recipe for the cocktail. The mugs are far rarer than Mule cups, but, curiously, much cheaper.

Flavor
Affinities:

There is also a recipe for a Harvey Wallbanger cake. There is something to be said for that, but no one is stepping forward to say it. Stick with spareribs and pupu platter–style appetizers.

Recipe:

Harvey Wallbanger:
1¹/₂ ounces vodka
6 ounces fresh orange juice
¹/₂ ounce Galliano

Pour the vodka and orange juice over ice in a chilled highball glass. Float the Galliano on top.

Variation:

Freddy Fudpucker:
Substitute tequila for the vodka, and say, "I beg your pardon?"

---

49. **HI HO COCKTAIL**

General
Description:

Originally made with sweeter Old Tom Gin (see page 24), the Hi Ho was an elegant twist on the Martini. Hollywood in the mid-1930s was celebrating the demise of one of the most unbearable plagues to descend upon Earth—Prohibition. Prior to Prohibition, cocktails had taken a turn toward ostentation. Perhaps it was the straightforwardness of gin or rye with ginger ale, or the modest cocktails served up at the classier speakeasies, but drinks entered a new age of simplicity and, subsequently, refinement following Prohibition. In this respect, the speakeasy was something of a rough stone waiting to be cut into the fine gem of the nightclub. The Hi Ho, from the Hi Ho Club in Hollywood, was a shining example of everything a cocktail should be. It was cold, crisp, and a pleasure to behold. The use of Old Tom Gin has just about sent this cocktail to the "endangered species list," but since London dry gin is being substituted these days, the Hi Ho may yet endure.

Purchase:

The bartenders who embrace tradition will happily shake up this snappy cocktail for you. Do not seek out the Hi Ho anywhere that has a "twofer" night.

Areas and Time of Occurrence:

The Brown Derby, the Roosevelt, the Embassy, and the Hi Ho Club of the 1930s are all gone, but the art of cocktail making lingers in the Hi Ho Cocktail. Get the tuxedos and cocktail dresses out of the mothballs, put on some Gershwin, and relive a bygone era.

Season:

Once again, a classic cocktail knows no season, but the Hi Ho is best suited to sipping under starlight.

Preparation:	This drink requires white port. While red port is much more common, white is readily available, and you should not compromise.
Flavor Affinities:	If you cannot afford caviar by the pound, smoked salmon or sturgeon canapés will fill in nicely. You may also want to pair the classic *bagna cauda*—a hot anchovy and garlic dip—with a medley of fresh crudités.
Recipe:	***Hi Ho Cocktail:*** **2 ounces gin** **1 ounce white port** **2 dashes of bitters** **Twist of lemon peel**

Shake the gin, white port, and bitters with ice; then strain into a chilled cocktail glass. Garnish with lemon peel.

HIGHBALL

General Description:	*A highball is any spirit served with a carbonated beverage over ice.* The origin of the term *highball* is about as difficult to pin down as a champagne bubble. New York bartender Patrick Duffy claimed to have invented it in 1895, and since no one has challenged him, he holds the title. A random poll in most bars would indicate that people have no idea what a highball is—

yet it is right in front of them. **Scotch and Soda**, **Gin and Tonic**, **Coolers**, **Daisies**, and so on are all highballs. A highball is primarily any alcoholic drink meant to refresh. The more common highballs are listed in their particular entries, but some noteworthy old and new options are presented here.

Purchase:

Apart from drinks that specifically have the word *highball* in their names, use of the term is generally archaic, but fun if you want to annoy or confuse people. "I'll have a Gin and Tonic highball" rolls off the tongue like a bowling ball.

Areas and Time of Occurrence:

From the last hole on the golf course to the front porch after mowing the lawn, from reading a newspaper after work to cooling off while tending the barbecue, a highball is a welcome reward.

Season:

No drink is more appreciated in any season than one of the countless highballs ready to be poured.

Preparation:

The highball is served in a highball glass, but that goes without saying. Mixing the drink into an old-fashioned glass makes it a lowball. "Build" the drink in the glass by slowly adding ingredients one at a time. Avoid overstirring freshly opened carbonated beverages. A flat highball is a foul ball.

| Flavor Affinities: | Since highballs are low-alcohol drinks that are sipped leisurely, consider an array of hearty appetizers, including broiled sausages, bacon-wrapped chicken livers, or ham and Swiss cheese cubes. |

| Recipes: | ***Basic Highball:***
1 ounce whiskey
Cold ginger ale
Twist of lemon peel |

Pour the whiskey into a chilled highball glass over ice. Add ginger ale to fill; then garnish with lemon peel.

Bermuda Highball:
³/₄ ounce gin
³/₄ ounce brandy
³/₄ ounce dry vermouth
Cold club soda or ginger ale
Twist of lemon peel

Pour the gin, brandy, and vermouth into a chilled highball glass over ice. Add soda to fill; then garnish with lemon peel.

Presbyterian:
2 ounces whiskey
2¹/₂ ounces club soda
2¹/₂ ounces cold ginger ale or 7-Up
Twist of lemon peel

Pour the whiskey, club soda, and ginger ale into a chilled highball glass over ice; then garnish with lemon peel.

Stone Fence:
2 ounces Scotch
2 dashes of bitters
Cold club soda or cider

 Pour the Scotch and bitters into a chilled highball glass over ice. Add soda to fill.

51a–c. **HOT TODDY**

General
Description:

A Hot Toddy is a general cool-weather glass of cheer with limitless combinations of spirits. Few ask whence the *toddy* in Hot Toddy comes. This is good, because nobody knows. The closest connection seems to be the name for the sap of an Asian palm tree, but no mention of this ingredient appears in the recipe. Some Hot Toddies, such as **Irish Coffee**, are listed in their particular entries, but others are here.

Purchase:

Although popular at ski resorts or inns, the Hot Toddy is not common in most cocktail lounges. This homey drink is best prepared at home.

Areas and Time
of Occurrence:

A blazing fire at dusk during a snowstorm was once the customary setting for sipping a Hot Toddy. While not as picturesque, a football game on a chilly after-noon is no less an appropriate backdrop for this soothing drink.

Season:

A cool evening requires no excuse to pour a Hot Toddy. The drink also serves as superb therapy for the last phases of early spring cabin fever.

Preparation:

Despite its name, the Hot Toddy should not be served too hot. Heat the mixture in a chafing dish or saucepan until just before boiling, and let it cool a few moments. For an added flair, you may also use a hot poker (see **Flip**).

Flavor Affinities:

Plan a Swedish-style smorgasbord of hot and cold appetizers.

Recipes:

Hot Toddy:
1 ounce brandy or rum
1 ounce honey
¹/₂ lemon slice studded with 2 cloves
Cinnamon stick (optional)

Combine the brandy, honey, and lemon slice in a mug or punch cup, and add hot water to fill. Stir with a cinnamon stick, if desired.

Hot Buttered Rum:
2 whole cloves

2 whole allspice berries
1 cinnamon stick
1 teaspoon sugar
2 ounces dark rum
1 teaspoon sweet butter
Freshly grated nutmeg

Combine the cloves, allspice, cinnamon stick, and sugar in a punch cup or mug, and add boiling water to fill. Let stand for 5 minutes; then add the rum and butter, and dust with nutmeg.

Mulled Wine:
1 teaspoon sugar
1 teaspoon fresh lemon juice
5 ounces red wine
Dash of bitters
Pinch each of nutmeg and cinnamon

Heat all ingredients in a saucepan until just under a boil. Cool slightly; then serve in a punch cup or mug.

 52. **HURRICANE**

General
Description:

The rum-based Hurricane is enlivened by passion fruit juice. The Hurricane may have been around before Pat O'Brien's French Quarter Bar began serving it in the 1930s, but it was that New Orleans institution that gave the drink its notoriety. The Hurricane was—and still is—so popular that the 26-ounce hurricane glass was created for it. The hurricane glass does bear an affinity to the hurricane lamp in shape, and those who imbibe two or three during Mardi Gras are certain to get all lit up.

Purchase:

Pat O'Brien's on St. Peter Street in the French Quarter is still the preeminent venue to sip one of these ruby-colored coolers.

Areas and Time of Occurrence:

If you cannot make it to the French Quarter, put some New Orleans jazz in the player, pour a round of Hurricanes, and watch the world glow just a little brighter. The Hurricane, like New Orleans itself, may be enjoyed at any time of the day—assuming you are civilized enough not to wake up before noon.

Season:

Mardi Gras may last only a short while, but the Hurricane can keep the spirit alive eternally.

Preparation:

Recipes vary as to the exact ingredients. Some call for contents amounting to a mere 3 ounces, but the norm is closer to 8 ounces, which goes a long way in a large hurricane glass filled with ice.

Flavor Affinities:

Take a tip from Pat O'Brien's, and cook up any of these lively appetizers: shrimp remoulade, hot wings, alligator bites, catfish strips, or crawfish nachos.

Recipe: ***Hurricane:***
1¹/₂ ounces dark rum
1¹/₂ ounces light rum
2 ounces passion fruit juice
1 ounce fresh lime juice
1 ounce unsweetened pineapple juice
1 teaspoon grenadine
1 teaspoon superfine sugar or simple syrup
Orange slice and maraschino cherry

Shake the two rums, the three juices, and the grenadine and sugar with ice; then strain into a chilled hurricane glass filled with ice. Garnish with an orange slice and a maraschino cherry.

53.   **IRISH COFFEE**

General
Description:

The original Irish Coffee was a concoction of a bit of whiskey, a generous splash of black coffee, a dollop of whipped cream, and a smattering of genius. Pedigrees for most drinks are dubious at best, but the Irish Coffee is well documented. *San Francisco Chronicle* columnist Stanton Delaplane was served one at Ireland's Shannon Airport bar in 1952; after returning to San Francisco, he passed the recipe on to barman Jack Koeppler at the Buena Vista and soon to the rest of the country. The story behind this immensely popular beverage is that Irish bartender Joe Sheridan created the rejuvenating brew during World War II to greet weary Yankee travelers arriving by seaplane in the wee hours of the morning. Interestingly, the Irish drank whiskey in tea, but Sheridan apparently knew the American palate and had the wherewithal to substitute coffee.

Purchase:

This is one drink you may be certain is available anywhere that has Irish whiskey and a coffee urn.

Areas and Time of Occurrence:

Irish pubs in those wee hours seem to be perennial havens for a last-call round of Irish Coffees. As the varieties of coffee increase, so do the occasions to drink it. Afternoon or early evening "coffee klatches" are becoming a new trend, and what better way to enliven a jolt of Joe but with a whit of whiskey?

Season:

Although one might instantly associate Irish Coffee with the cooler months, it should really have no more seasonal boundaries than coffee itself.

Preparation:

The best Irish Coffee should be treated no differently than the naked brew. Use high-quality, freshly ground and brewed beans, and always whip your heavy cream without sugar right before serving.

Flavor Affinities:

As an afternoon beverage, Irish Coffee may be served with mini quiches or an assortment of pastries.

Recipe: ***Irish Coffee:***
4 ounces freshly brewed coffee
1¹/₂ ounces Irish whiskey
1 teaspoon brown sugar
Dollop of freshly whipped cream

Combine the coffee, whiskey, and sugar in a hot Irish coffee mug; then float whipped cream on top.

Variations: ***Italian Coffee:***
Substitute amaretto for the whiskey.

Jamaican Coffee:
Substitute dark rum for the whiskey.

Mexican Coffee:
Substitute Kahlúa for the whiskey.

54a–b.   **JELL-O SHOT**

General
Description: *Originally made from vodka and flavored gelatin, Jell-O Shots are traditionally served in tiny paper cups.* Jell-O Shots—you either love them, or you excoriate them. James Audubon listed all the birds he encountered for the sake of completion, and Jell-O Shots are therefore included here. Of course, Audubon stuffed his birds in order to draw them, and that fate is wished upon the Jell-O Shot by many traditionalists. William

Grimes in *Straight Up or On the Rocks* vilifies them as "abominations." But "sucking slime," as it is known to its devotees, is probably the best way to catch up on your Jell-O if no hospital visit is in sight. These thing-a-ma-jiggles are also perfect party treats for those who arrive late and want to get as dead drunk as everyone else in no time at all.

Purchase:

Unless you know of a bar that specializes in these squiggly dainties, prepare them at home.

Areas and Time of Occurrence:

Posh, swanky, and debonair. These words have nothing whatsoever to do with Jell-O Shots—unless you consider catching them in your mouth at the bar the way a dolphin catches fish to be posh, swanky, and debonair. Being highly portable potables, they may be transported to your favorite parking lots, alleys, and laundromats. Jimmy Buffett music is a must.

Season:

The Jell-O Shot may lean toward summer, but it also makes a natural spring break pastime.

Preparation:

If you possess the culinary prowess to make Jell-O, you will master these little globs in no time. Ways to serve this treat are limited only by your imagination and by the varied supply of Jell-O flavors. Opinions vary minimally on the proper way to serve Jell-O Shots, and connoisseurs will assure you that the most fitting manner is in small paper cups. Experts will point out that these cups are easily appropriated from the condiment counter of any major fast-food establishment.

Flavor
Affinities:
Being a form of comestible, the Jell-O Shot requires no specific food. If you're hungry, however, serve what you normally would with Jell-O. If on a binge, Lucky Charms or ambrosia would cure any craving.

Recipe:
Jell-O Shot:
I package Jell-O flavored gelatin
6 ounces boiling water
6 ounces vodka, gin, or anything else

Pour the gelatin into a bowl; then add the boiling water, and stir until the gelatin dissolves. Add the vodka, stir, and pour into an ice cube tray or molds of your choice. Refrigerate until set. This batch will serve one heroic individual, or ten curious ones a shot each.

Variations:
General Knox:
(From a barman called Seafarer John)
Use unflavored gelatin and a Martini blend in place of straight vodka.

Lava Lamp:
Drop Jell-O Shots in a glass of cold vodka.

55.   **LEAP YEAR COCKTAIL**

General
Description:

*The mixture of gin and vermouth gives the Leap Year Cocktail a certain affinity to a **Martini**, but the addition of Grand Marnier makes this cocktail unique.* Gary Regan in his book *The Joy of Mixology* states that Harry Craddock of the Savoy Bar in London created the Leap Year Cocktail to celebrate February 29, 1928. *The Savoy Cocktail Book* insists that this drink has been "responsible for more proposals than any other cocktail that has ever been mixed." Begging pardon, but February 29 is also Sadie Hawkins Day, which may have something to do with this mass plunge into wedlock.

Purchase:

This drink becomes a special at many bars on February 29 but is then forgotten for the next four years. The Leap Year is a cocktail that bartenders would be happy to make for you if they knew what it was. Order it by its ingredients.

Areas and Time
of Occurrence:

Perhaps the Leap Year Cocktail was created with a particular date in mind, but those not yet practiced in the grab-you-by-your-boot-straps dryness of a Martini may want to sample this elegant alternative. The Grand Marnier makes this cocktail a top-shelf drink not particularly suited to bars that open before seven in the morning.

Season: Despite being associated with February, a nicely chilled Leap Year Cocktail is appropriate any time.

Preparation: Use the Martini as your rule of thumb, and shake or stir as you see fit.

Flavor Affinities: Enjoy a Leap Year with oysters with garlic tarragon crust in the winter, or with goat cheese crisp or crudités and green goddess dip during the summer.

Recipe: ***Leap Year Cocktail:***
2 ounces gin
¹/₂ ounce Grand Marnier
¹/₄ ounce fresh lemon juice
Twist of lemon peel

Shake the gin, Grand Marnier, and lemon juice with ice; then strain into a chilled cocktail glass. Garnish with lemon peel.

56a–b. **LEMON DROP**

General Description: *The Lemon Drop is a vodka-based cocktail that contrasts the sweetness of sugar with the tartness of lemon.* Most likely named for the candy, the Lemon Drop has undergone a number of revisions over the years. It has been both a cocktail and a shooter, and the ingredients have also changed. Whatever its incarnation, the

Color Plates

Icon Key

PREPARATION

bar spoon	blender	boiling water
bottle opener	bowl of water	cocktail shaker
corkscrew	frying pan	heat
knife	muddler	pitcher

PREPARATION (continued)		
reamer	refrigerate	tap water
vegetable peeler	waiting required	

GARNISHES		
cherry	ice	olive
slice	twist	wedge

GLASSWARE

brandy snifter	beer glass/mug	champagne flute
cocktail	collins	cordial
highball	hurricane	margarita
mug	old fashioned	pousse café

GLASSWARE (continued)			
punch bowl	shot	sherry	sour
SEASON			
spring	summer	fall	winter
TIME OF DAY		MISCELLANEOUS	
morning	night	endangered species	photo

1. **absinthe drip**

2. **adonis**

3a. **brandy alexander**

3b. **alexander's sister**

3c. parisian blond

4. algonquin

5. american beauty

6. americano

7. **añejo highball**

8a. **amer picon cocktail**

8b. **french kiss**

8c. **kir**

8d. **lillet cocktail**

8e. **seething jealousy**

9a. **applejack cocktail**

9b. **jack rose cocktail**

10. **apricot cocktail**

11. **aviation cocktail**

12. **bacardi cocktail**

13a. **black velvet**

13b. depth charge

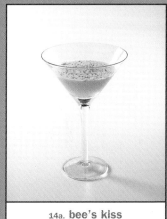

14a. bee's kiss

14b. bee's knees

15. bellini

16a. **black russian**

16b. **white russian**

17. **bloody mary**

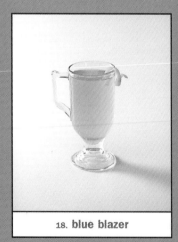

18. **blue blazer**

19a. **brown derby**

19b. **horse's neck**

19c. **bourbonella**

20a. **brandy crusta**

20b. **bosom caresser**

20c. **brandy gump**

21a. **bronx**

21b. **brooklyn**

22. **caipirinha**

23a. **cape codder**

23b. **bay breeze**

23c. **sea breeze**

23d. **madras**

24a. **champagne cocktail**

24b. **mimosa**

24c. **kir royale**

25a. **clover club cocktail**

25b. **honeymoon cocktail**

25c. **maiden's prayer**

25d. **pegu club cocktail**

25e. **satan's whiskers**

26a. **basic brandy cobbler**

26b. **irish fix**

26c. **cherry cobbler**

27a. **basic cooler**

27b. **floradora cooler**

27c. **campari cooler**

28a. **alabama slammer**

28b. **golden dream**

28c. **horny leprechaun**

28d. **silent monk**

29a. **basic cosmopolitan**

29b. **metropolitan**

29c. **neopolitan**

30a. **black lung (smokers)**

30b. **black lung (nonsmokers)**

30c. **peanut butter cuptini**

31. **cuba libre (rum and coke)**

32a. **classic daiquiri**

32b. **hemingway daiquiri**

32c. classic frozen daiquiri

32d. frozen banana daiquiri

33. gin daisy

34a. dubonnet cocktail (zaza)

34b. **lady madonna**

35a. **the unitini**

35b. **oyster martini**

36a. **flip**

36b. **hot brandy flip**

37a. **all white frappé**

37b. **banana rum frappé**

38a. **blue berkeley**

38b. **smooth operator**

38c. **frozen apple**

39a. **fuzzy navel**

39b. **WOO WOO**

40. **gimlet**

41. **classic gin and tonic**

42a. **gin and it**

42b. **gin and sin**

42c. **pink gin**

43a. **gin fizz**

43b. **ramos gin fizz**

43c. **sloe gin fizz**

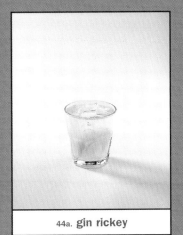

44a. gin rickey

44b. cosmo rickey

45a. girl scout cookie

45b. almond joy

46a. **godfather**

46b. **reservoir dog**

46c. **gone with the wind**

47a. **traditional grog**

47b. **grog cocktail**

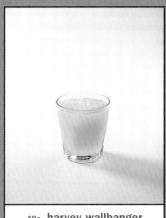

48a. **harvey wallbanger**

48b. **freddy fudpucker**

49. **hi ho cocktail**

50a. **basic highball**

50b. **bermuda highball**

50c. **stone fence**

51a. **hot toddy**

51b. hot buttered rum

51c. mulled wine

52. hurricane

53. irish coffee

54a. **jell-o shot**

54b. **lava lamp**

55. **leap year cocktail**

56a. **lemon drop 1**

56b. **lemon drop 2**

57. **liquid cocaine 1**

58a. **long island iced tea**

58b. **california lemonade**

58c. **electric iced tea**

58d. **root beer**

59a. **mai tai**

59b. **suffering bastard**

60. **manhattan**

61a. **margarita**

61b. **blue margarita**

61c. **frozen margarita**

62a. **martini (1)**

62b. **martini (2)**

62c. **the gibson**

62d. **blue martini**

62e. **dirty martini**

62f. **naked martini**

63a. **mary pickford**

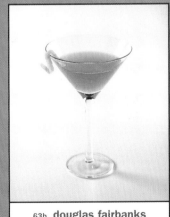

63b. **douglas fairbanks**

63c. **garbo gargle cocktail**

63d. **mae west**

64. **mint julep**

65. **mojito**

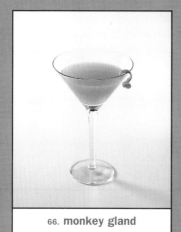

66. **monkey gland**

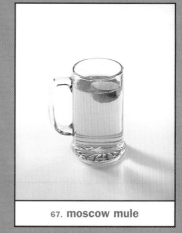

67. **moscow mule**

68. **negroni**

69. **classic old fashioned**

70. **orange blosson**

71. **paris is burning**

72a. **savoy corpse reviver**

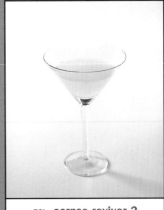

72b. **corpse reviver 2**

72c. **prairie oyster**

73. **pimm's cup**

74. **piña colada**

75a. **pink lady**

75b. **pink panther**

76a. **abc**

76b. **angel's kiss**

76c. **b-52**

76d. chocolate-covered cherry

76e. mexican flag

76f. slippery nipple

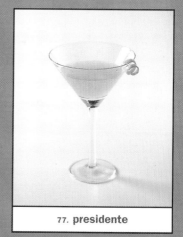

77. presidente

78a. **artillery punch**

78b. **eggnog**

78c. **planter's punch cocktail**

79. **rob roy**

80a. **a day at the beach**

80b. **bahama mama**

80c. **black maria**

80d. **blue hawaii**

80e. **bolero**

80f. **continental**

80g. **havana cocktail**

80h. **lounge lizard**

81. **rusty nail**

82a. **approve**

82b. old nick

82c. opening

83. sangria

84. sazerac

85a. **affinity**

85b. **bobby burns**

85c. **debonair**

85d. **scotch and soda**

86a. **screwdriver**

86b. **melon ball**

86c. **southern screw**

87a. **sex on the beach**

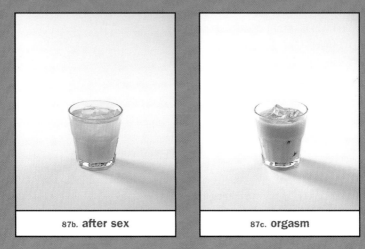

87b. **after sex**

87c. **orgasm**

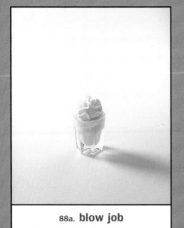

88a. **blow job**

88b. **kamikaze**

89a. **sidecar**

89b. **between the sheets**

89c. **bmw sidecar**

90a. **singapore sling**

90b. **gin sling**

91. **whiskey sour**

92a. **stinger**

92b. **grasshopper**

92c. scorpion

92d. tarantula

93. rum swizzle

94a. brave bull

94b. **hot pants**

94c. **silk stockings**

94d. **tequila mockingbird**

95. **tequila sunrise**

96. tom collins

97a. blue lagoon

97b. desert sunrise

97c. salty dog

97d. **dusty dog**

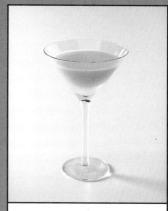

97e. **road runner**

97f. **hazy days of winter**

98a. **vodka martini (stalini)**

98b. **french martini**

98c. **apple martini**

98d. **chocolate martini**

99. **ward eight**

100. **scotch and water**

101a. **broken spur**

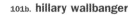

101b. **hillary wallbanger**

101c. **white wine spritzer**

102. zombie

drink is meant to go down smooth—so smooth that it has a way of creeping up on you and bashing you on the noggin with a brickbat. The Lemon Drop seems to date from the archetypal singles bars—the so-called fern bars—of the late 1960s. With their puffy couches, Tiffany-style lamps, and laid-back atmosphere, fern bars capitalized on the Age of Aquarius and thrived until Hard Rock Cafes lured away their trendy clientele. Like many not-so-legal stimulants of the time, the aim of the Lemon Drop was peace, harmony, and insensibility. Current variations have since put the drink more in league with the **Cosmopolitan**.

Purchase: This cocktail is growing in popularity and turning up in all of the bars "of the moment," but it is also a simple drink to mix at home.

Areas and Time of Occurrence: There is no need to dredge out the headbands or the Iron Butterfly album, because the Lemon Drop is just as at home with a DKNY skirt and Michael Bublé. Order a Lemon Drop when you are out at night and in the mood for a cold but slightly sweet cocktail.

Season: As much of a summertime drink as this seems to be, Gary and Mardee Regan in *New Classic Cocktails* recall tasting their first Lemon Drops as shooters on Christmas Day in 1991.

Preparation: Try to avoid making the drink too sweet. It can also
                be sipped like straight tequila by downing a sugar-
                rimmed shot glass of cold citrus vodka followed by
                biting into a lemon wedge.

Flavor   Because it tends to be rather sweet, pair the Lemon
Affinities: Drop with salty blue cheese dip, gravlax, or ceviche.

Recipes: ***Lemon Drop 1:***
                Sugar for rimming
                3 ounces lemon-infused (citron) vodka
                1 ounce freshly squeezed lemon juice
                Lemon wedge

Rim a chilled cocktail glass lightly with lemon juice
and sugar. Shake the vodka and lemon juice with ice;
then strain into the cocktail glass. Garnish with a
lemon wedge.

Lemon Drop 2:
Sugar for rimming
2¹/₂ ounces lemon-infused (citron) vodka
¹/₂ ounce Cointreau or triple sec
¹/₂ ounce freshly squeezed lemon juice
Lemon wedge

Rim a chilled cocktail glass with sugar. Shake the
vodka, Cointreau, and lemon juice with ice; then strain
into the cocktail glass. Garnish with a lemon wedge.

57.   **LIQUID COCAINE**

General
Description:

The name and purpose of Liquid Cocaine are far more important than what ingredients are used. This infamous cocktail might not have required its own entry, except that it has hatched so many variations that it deserves one. In spite of the oft-called-for ingredient Rumple Minze, Liquid Cocaine does not "mince" words. This is a drink that is meant to get you somewhere—even if you don't know where that is beforehand and don't recall where it was afterward. Liquid Cocaine is one drink where the sum is not equal to its parts. With 151-proof rum commonly called for, the equation rarely works out right.

Purchase:

Judging from the place names appended to Liquid Cocaine—Chicago-Style, Northwest-Style, and so on—this very potent potable is universal. Bid the bartender "good night" before you start drinking.

Areas and Time
of Occurrence:

Look for bars with bartenders who have pointed tails protruding from under their clothing. When **Jell-O Shots** just don't have their pop, mix one of these.

Season:

Since you won't care what season it is after you have downed a couple, it shouldn't matter.

Preparation:

Liquid Cocaine is served over ice or as a shooter. The key is that this liquidator be drunk very cold.

Flavor Affinities:	The mélange of spirits in Liquid Cocaine defies food pairings. Stick with Chex Mix, pretzels, and other bar carbs—before the bicarb.

Recipes:

Liquid Cocaine 1:
¹/₂ ounce 151-proof rum
¹/₂ ounce Rumple Minze
¹/₂ ounce Jägermeister
¹/₂ ounce Goldschlager

Shake all ingredients with ice; then strain over ice into a chilled old-fashioned glass. Alternatively, put the liquor in the freezer, and serve neat in a shot glass.

Liquid Cocaine 2:
¹/₂ ounce 151-proof rum
¹/₂ ounce vodka
¹/₂ ounce amaretto
¹/₂ ounce Frangelico

Shake all ingredients with ice; then strain over ice into a chilled old-fashioned glass. Alternatively, put the liquor in the freezer, and serve neat in a shot glass.

58a–d.

LONG ISLAND ICED TEA

General Description:	*The Long Island Iced Tea is one of many creative cocktails whose numerous ingredients are intended to simu-*

late the flavor of something entirely different. Although definitely not tea nor containing any tea, the Long Island Iced Tea does taste like tea, and it did hail from Long Island. Robert C. "Rosebud" Butt is credited with creating this drink in the 1970s; ever since, he has been toast of the town as well as the butt of many diatribes. As Joseph Scott and Donald Bain point out in *The World's Best Bartender Guide*, the problem with the Long Island Iced Tea is that it doesn't taste like an alcoholic drink, and therefore those otherwise circumspect about drinking alcohol summarily end up as boiled as an owl. In fact, two's the limit in most bars, and other bars will no longer serve it because it goes down so easily—and soon the drinker follows suit.

Still, the Long Island Iced Tea need not be a knockout punch. By halving the ingredients, the flavor remains but the kick is softened. A bevy of creative cocktails have been inspired by the LIIT's creative side to replicate other flavors, while others are just an excuse to get you rapidly snozzled. This entry lists some of both. Perhaps the most unusual is the Pan Galactic Gargle Blaster, a cocktail that has its basis in fiction. The original Pan Galactic Gargle Blaster was described by Douglas Adams in his *Hitchhiker's Guide to the Galaxy*. It was a potent drink invented by Zaphod Beeblebrox, and the effects have been likened to "having your brains smashed out with a slice of lemon wrapped round a large gold brick." Bartenders who have attempted to reproduce this drink using more earthbound ingredients are dedicated to equaling Adams's goal.

Purchase:
The Long Island Iced Tea is usually ordered out because of its number of ingredients. Since the components of this drink should be in every basic bar, however, you can just as easily, and wisely, shake these up at home.

Areas and Time of Occurrence:
☾
Originally an American frat house formulation, the Long Island Iced Tea has made its way in and out of bars and lounges across the country, inspiring adherents and detractors along the way. While not intended to be a nightcap, it nevertheless has a way of abruptly and unceremoniously putting an end to an evening.

Season:
❄ ☀ ❀ ❄
The Long Island Iced Tea has the same season as regular iced tea. If you like iced tea in the dead of winter, there should be nothing to stop you from making its alcoholic relative.

Preparation:
Harmony and balance are central to a Long Island Iced Tea. Substituting ingredients or changing proportions will only give you a Long Island Expressway traffic jam.

Flavor Affinities:
Basic bar grub goes well with a Long Island Iced Tea. Jalapeño poppers, onion rings, nachos, and burgers are all suitable.

Recipe: **_Long Island Iced Tea:_**
¹/₂ ounce vodka
¹/₂ ounce gin
¹/₂ ounce tequila
¹/₂ ounce light rum
¹/₂ ounce fresh lemon juice
¹/₂ ounce triple sec
1 teaspoon superfine sugar
Cold cola
Wedge of lemon

Shake the vodka, gin, tequila, rum, lemon juice, triple sec, and sugar with ice; then strain into a chilled collins glass filled with ice. Add cola to fill, gently stir, and garnish with a lemon wedge.

Variations: **_California Lemonade:_**
Juice of 1 large lemon
Juice of 1 large lime
1 teaspoon superfine sugar
2 ounces Scotch
¹/₄ teaspoon grenadine
Cold club soda
Wedge of lemon

Shake the lemon juice, lime juice, sugar, Scotch, and grenadine with ice; then strain into a chilled collins glass filled with ice. Add soda to fill, gently stir, and garnish with a lemon wedge.

Texas Tea:
Add ¹/₂ ounce bourbon.

Electric Iced Tea:
¹/₂ ounce vodka
¹/₂ ounce gin
¹/₂ ounce bourbon
¹/₂ ounce fresh lemon juice
¹/₂ ounce triple sec
Cold lemon-lime soda
Wedge of lemon

Shake the vodka, gin, bourbon, lemon juice, and triple sec with ice; then strain into a chilled collins glass filled with ice. Add soda to fill, gently stir, and garnish with a lemon wedge.

Root Beer:
1 ounce Galliano
1 ounce Kahlúa
Cold cola

Shake the Galliano and Kahlúa well with ice; then strain into a chilled collins glass filled with ice. Add cola to fill.

Pan Galactic Gargle Blaster:
The original recipe calls for Arcturan Mega gin, Qualactin Hypermint extract, Algolian Suntiger, and

Zamphuor, but they are not readily available yet.

1¹/₂ ounces vodka
1¹/₂ ounces light rum
1¹/₂ ounces Southern Comfort
¹/₂ ounce 151-proof rum
6 ounces cranberry juice
Wedge of lemon

Shake the vodka, light rum, Southern Comfort, 151-proof rum, and cranberry juice vigorously with ice; then strain into a chilled collins glass filled with ice. Garnish with a lemon wedge and, in Adams's words, "Drink . . . but . . . very carefully."

59a–b.

MAI TAI

General
Description:

The Mai Tai is a sweet-and-sour cocktail with fruit flavors balancing aged rum. All agree that "Trader Vic" Bergeron mixed the first Mai Tai in 1944 at his Hinky Dink bar in Emeryville, California, just outside of San Francisco. Naysayers need only heed the words of Trader Vic's bartenders' guide of 1947: "Anybody who says I didn't create this drink is a dirty stinker." Trader Vic had visited the South Seas, returning with all of the venerable accoutrements now standard in a tiki lounge. He created the drink for two friends, Eastham and Carrie Guild, who were visiting from Tahiti and requested something special from the bar. After taking a sip, Carrie said "Mai tai—ro aé," which translates from Tahitian as "Out of this world—the best." Like the "Polynesian" food Trader Vic served in his restaurant, the drink was completely ersatz as a South Seas libation. But it caught on, and apart from being out of this world, the Mai Tai is now one of the world's classic drinks.

Purchase:

Unlike other classic cocktails that require expertise, the sweetness of a Mai Tai covers up many a slight mistake. Because of its unusual ingredients, this is one drink that even bartenders generally order out.

Areas and Time
of Occurrence:

When you find yourself amid giant conch shells, carved masks, tiki gods, and thatched roofing, a Mai Tai is surely nearby. If you can't make it to the shore, put *South Pacific* or Les Baxter's music on and toast the crimson setting sun.

Season:

Whatever the season, the Mai Tai transports you to summer in the South Seas.

Preparation:

Trader Vic originally used seventeen-year-old rum in his recipe, you may substitute a blend of dark and light rum, or just light rum. A Mai Tai is too busy having too much of a good time to argue.

Flavor
Affinities:

Regarding food, Trader Vic said, "You can't eat real Polynesian food. It's the most horrible stuff I've ever tasted." As with certain people who hate broccoli, we disagree. For fun's sake, pile the tables with fresh pineapples and bananas, dim sum, and that pupu platter you always wanted to order.

Recipe:

Mai Tai:
2 ounces aged rum
1 ounce Cointreau or triple sec
¹/₂ ounce grenadine
1 teaspoon orgeat
1 ounce fresh lime juice
Tropical fruit, such as pineapple, kiwi, or citrus

Shake the rum, Cointreau, grenadine, orgeat, and lime juice well with ice; then strain into a chilled hurricane glass filled with ice. Garnish with fresh fruit and one of those little umbrellas.

Variation:

Suffering Bastard:
Substitute light and dark rum for the aged rum, omit the grenadine, and add 2 ounces fresh orange juice.

60.

MANHATTAN

General Description:

The Manhattan is the quintessential blend of straight rye whiskey and vermouth, rounded out by bitters. With the diminishing presence of rye since Prohibition, bourbon has supplanted it. If the mundane is your cup of tea,

believe this story of origin: a saloon keeper on the
Lower East Side looked out the window of his establishment and named this preeminently classic cocktail
for Manhattan Island. If your tastes tend to the more
colorful, go with this one: Jennie Churchill—the
bibulous Winston's American mother—hosted a party
at New York's Manhattan Club in 1874 to celebrate
the newly elected governor William J. Tilden. The
anonymous bartender honored both Tilden and the
club by christening the new drink the Manhattan.
The only other story in the running was also generated
from the same locale but for a different person. The
year was 1890, and the instigator in this case was
Supreme Court justice Charles Henry Truax. According
to James Villas in *Villas at Table*, Truax's daughter
claims that Truax asked a Manhattan Club bartender
to mix him up a new drink because his doctor told
him to stop imbibing **Martinis** if he wanted to lose
weight. The doctor's credentials, as far as we know,
have never been challenged on the caloric qualities of
Martinis versus Manhattans.

Manhattans may be served sweet, perfect, or dry,
with blended whiskey or bourbon, but the original
was mixed with rye. The cocktail immediately sup-
plied the well-heeled with a sophisticated way to slug
down whiskey. The Manhattan will never overtake the
Martini's status, but it must be heralded alongside its
gin counterpart in the peerage of great classic cocktails.
On a final historical note, Tilden won the popular

vote for the U.S. presidency in 1876 but lost in the electoral. It makes one wonder what Al Gore is drinking these days.

Purchase: The Manhattan has never gone out of fashion in traditional bars and hotels, but according to many young bartenders, the Manhattan is now making its way to the trendier bar scene—albeit with bourbon, not rye. This is definitely one drink you need to know how to make as a home bartender. No excuses.

Areas and Time of Occurrence: The Manhattan has always been associated with black-tie affairs, wood-paneled bars, and the fox-trot. Bette Midler's ordering a Manhattan in the Tom Waits duet "I Never Talk to Strangers" gave it a renewed legitimacy with the younger generation. Bars that emulate the swank atmosphere of erstwhile nightclubs have been quick to include the Manhattan as the new old drink of the moment.

Season: Oddly, the Manhattan is not as much of a year-round drink as one might expect. Sales tend to rise from fall to late spring.

Preparation: The Manhattan was conceived with rye as its essential component, but the consensus is that even if you don't use rye, Manhattans should be made with American whiskey, such as a good bourbon. In fact, if you use Scotch, you will have created a **Rob Roy**. The

Manhattan has its shaker and stirrer adherents, but the debate is nowhere as rancorous as the Martini's. The major defense for shaking a Martini is that it be teeth-chatteringly cold. That is not the case with the Manhattan, but shaking does impart a momentary frothiness that some find appealing. A classic Manhattan requires a maraschino cherry.

Flavor
Affinities:

Salty and peppery hors d'oeuvres complement the sweet edge of the Manhattan. Try briny caviar on toast points, carpaccio, and a cheese board.

Recipe:

Manhattan:
2 ounces straight rye or bourbon
1 ounce sweet vermouth
Dash of Angostura bitters
Maraschino cherry

Stir the bourbon, vermouth, and bitters in a pitcher half filled with ice, or shake them with ice; then strain into a chilled cocktail glass. Garnish with a maraschino cherry.

Variations:

Dry Manhattan:
Substitute dry vermouth for the sweet vermouth, and garnish with a twist of lemon peel.

Perfect Manhattan:
Substitute half dry and half sweet vermouth for the

sweet vermouth, and garnish with a twist of lemon peel or a maraschino cherry.

Tequila Manhattan:

Substitute tequila for the whiskey, use only half the sweet vermouth, and garnish with a maraschino cherry.

61a–c.

MARGARITA

General Description:

The Margarita is a cocktail made from tequila, Cointreau or triple sec, and lime juice. Despite its few ingredients, the drink is further proof that in a classic cocktail, less is more. With the number of people claiming the invention of the Margarita around the same time, it is more likely that the time was right for a darned good idea. Considering the few ingredients it calls for, it's surprising that the Margarita wasn't invented sooner. Among the claimants for the drink's creation are Doña Bertha, owner of Bertita's Bar in Tasca, Mexico; Daniel Negrete of the Crespí Hotel in Puebla, Mexico; Pancho Morales of Tommy's Place in Juárez; and Mariano Martinez of Dallas's El Charro. Martinez's son further asserted that he made the first frozen Margarita in 1971. Then there is the legion of Margarets, Marjories, and Margaritas for which the drink is said to have been named. Tack on the innumerable individualized recipes, personal touches, and variations, and one may hypothesize that the Margarita is like a snowflake—no two are exactly alike.

Of course, one may ask how the Margarita caught on at all. Tequila, and consequently the Margarita, did not become common outside Latin America until the second half of the 1900s. It is amazing what a little triple sec and lime can do. Unfortunately, few classic cocktails have been as debased by the use of prefab mixes, degraded by being squirted out of hose guns, and anesthetized into frozen soda pop as the Margarita has. Purists bemoan the devolution of the Margarita, and some bars refuse to serve it frozen. The most cutting blow may have occurred in 2001 when a 7,000-gallon "Big Rita" erected at the Phloridays Parrothead Phestival in Orlando earned the title of World's Largest Cocktail in the *Guinness Book of World Records*. It would seem that that the perpetrators knew as much about cocktails as they did about spelling.

Purchase:

Purchase Margaritas only from bars or lounges where you know they make them on the spot. If you can watch the bartender squeeze fresh limes, much the better. This is another essential cocktail to learn how to make at home.

Areas and Time of Occurrence:

From taquerías and singles' bars to baseball games and garden parties, the Margarita is everywhere. Any bar with the word "parrot" as part of its name will probably make a decent Margarita. Do not look for Margaritas at food courts in shopping malls—unless the bar has the word "parrot" in its name. All-you-can-drink Margarita nights are also out.

Season:

The Margarita may have started as a warm-weather drink, but its enticing disposition has given it enduring appeal year-round.

Preparation:

Never use a mix, unless you want to make a Margarita incorrectly. Along with being fresh, a Margarita must be served cold enough for your throat to say hello to it on the way down. And at all costs, steer clear of plastic glasses, however cool looking.

Flavor Affinities:

The Margarita is often associated with nachos and quesadillas, but you can upgrade those bar standards by making your nachos with chile-rubbed sirloin and your quesadillas with radicchio and manchego cheese.

Recipe:

Margarita:
Wedge of lime and coarse or sea salt for rimming
2 ounces tequila
³/₄ ounce fresh lime juice
1 ounce Cointreau or triple sec
Wedge of lime

Rim a margarita glass with lime and salt, and chill briefly. Shake the tequila, lime juice, and Cointreau with ice; then strain into the chilled glass. Add ice if desired. Garnish with a lime wedge.

Variations:

Blue Margarita:
Add 3/4 ounce blue curaçao.

Chile Rita:
Made from an infusion of 15 jalapeño peppers steeped in a bottle of tequila for five days, the resulting fiery liquor is used in place of the regular tequila.

Mezcal Margarita:
Substitute mezcal for the tequila.

Frozen Margarita:
Place the ingredients along with 2 teaspoons superfine sugar or simple syrup and about a cup of cracked ice in a blender, and process until frothy.

Frozen Strawberry Margarita:
Place the ingredients along with 2 teaspoons superfine sugar or simple syrup, 1/2 cup chopped fresh strawberries, and about a cup of cracked ice in a blender, and process until frothy.

62a–f.

MARTINI

General Description:

*The Martini is made with gin and vermouth and is garnished with a twist of lemon peel or an olive—period. The **Vodkatini** has made a reputation for itself in its own right and is therefore discussed in a separate entry.*

King Arthur's knights searched in vain for the Holy Grail. The Spaniards sought the gold of El Dorado and the longevity of the Fountain of Youth. Lieutenant Gerard hunted Richard Kimble in *The Fugitive*. There is another modern quest, however, that has generated as much zeal and excitement: the search for the "perfect Martini." Armed with sterling silver shakers, vermouth droppers, and plenty of attitude and individuality, home bartenders mix and experiment with their Martinis with alchemical precision. Meanwhile, devoted seekers of the perfect Martini will flock to touted cocktail lounges like pilgrims to a revered shrine. It is a paradox indeed that the quintessential cocktail is so elusive.

The origin of the Martini is also as elusive as the Grail itself. The controversy over who sired the first one spans the colorful to the prosaic, and we may never know if this "elixir of quietude," "silver bullet," and "Fred Astaire in a glass" was named for a man, a rifle, or a vermouth producer. Whether named for a thirsty traveler on his way to Martinez or for Martini di Arma di Taggia, bartender at the Knickerbocker Hotel in New York City, the Martini is recognized as the world's premier cocktail; its stylized icon for the cocktail lounge is as universally recognizable as the symbol for the stop sign.

Many excellent books detail the history and evolution of the Martini and rhapsodize its lore, so it will only be necessary to touch upon a few highlights here.

It should immediately be noted that the early versions of the cocktail—Jerry Thomas's Martinez of 1887; Harry Johnson's Martini Cocktail of 1888; and di Taggia's version from the early twentieth century— were all super-sweet Neanderthals compared to today's bone-dry descendants. Thomas called for sweetened Old Tom gin, maraschino liqueur, and a whopping wine glass of Italian vermouth, and even di Taggia mixed equal parts gin and vermouth. During Prohibition, the Martini gradually saw the diminishing of its sweet ingredients and a turn toward dryness. By the end of World War II, the Martini was reaching a ratio of eight to one, and everyone you know probably has some joke about how to make a dry Martini (see below). Bernard DeVoto, whose book *The Hour* is a paean to the Martini, proclaimed the Martini to be the "supreme American gift to world culture"; H. L. Mencken pronounced it "the only American invention as perfect as a sonnet."

But the sonnet was in jeopardy in the 1970s when President Jimmy Carter denounced the "three-Martini lunch," and a sudden health craze cast out the Martini like a contagious leper. A critic in *Esquire* magazine railed that the drink was a bitter, medicinal-tasting beverage that stood for everything from phony bourgeois values and social snobbery to jaded alcoholism and latent masochism. Though it seemed headed for the funeral pyre, the Martini reemerged from the flames and has become virtually irreproachable.

On a closing note, there is a moment in Ernest Hemingway's *A Farewell to Arms* when the ex-soldier Frederic Henry celebrates his escape from the war with a satisfying meal. While eating he deliberates, "The sandwiches came and I ate three and drank a couple more martinis. I had never tasted anything so cool and lean. They made me feel civilized."

Purchase: Everyone makes the perfect Martini. Asking just for a Martini at a bar, however, is like asking for a glass of white wine. To avoid any disappointments, describe exactly how you like yours made. This is difficult with acquaintances, because telling a compatriot how to fix a Martini is a prelude to disaster, if not a broken nose.

Areas and Time of Occurrence: As many business deals are discussed over a Martini as are sweet nothings. Martinis are sipped in bars to the strains of Cole Porter, Diana Krall, and the Gipsy Kings and imbibed at French discothèques to the beat of chill-out lounge music. The lunchtime Martini may have been challenged, but no one has questioned the venerable cocktail hour. For DeVoto, that is the time when the Martini is "the healer, the weaver of forgiveness and reconciliation, the justifier of us to ourselves and one another." The Martini is urbane and urban. It is not a drink for the hayloft or the hoe-down. The Martini is best sipped where there is a view: the broad expanse of a city beneath you or just your lovely partner seated across the table.

Season:

As unique as it is, the Martini embraces all seasons and is served daily by some as an unfaltering ritual. Churchill mixed precisely two a day, no more, no less—or so he said.

Preparation:

Many opinions exist as to what makes for a perfect Martini—probably more opinions than there are people. This is in small part due to the schizophrenic age in which we live, and to a larger degree to the ruminations made after pondering the empty glass of a second Martini. Shaking or stirring is a personal preference (see "Technique," page 19). For every adept who stirs, another shakes. The fact remains, however, that shaking will get the Martini colder. And if you stir, larger ice cubes will need to be stirred longer than smaller ones. There are also those who complain that shaking bruises the gin. That gin can be bruised in the first place has some folks scratching their heads. Gin cannot be bruised.

Another issue is whether to keep gin in the freezer for optimum coldness. Some people swear by this, while others practically swear at it. The latter camp argues that gin should not be kept in the freezer because it will not dilute properly when mixed with ice. Try it both ways; you will undoubtedly agree that the best Martinis are made with gin kept in the freezer. Vermouth should be kept in the fridge, if only to prolong shelf life. With the dry Martinis of today, a bottle of vermouth may last almost as long as a bottle of bitters. Whether to include olives—whole, pitted, or stuffed with pimiento—or whether to squeeze a twist of lemon peel into the drink is a matter of choice. Chill standard-size cocktail glasses in the freezer (see "Glassware," page 12).

If one point is unanimously agreed upon, it is that a Martini should be dry. The amount of vermouth is negligible at best and will hardly alter the amount of alcohol in the cocktail glass. So, how do you keep your Martini dry? One suggestion is that you use an atomizer for the vermouth, but just be certain it's clean! Another suggestion is that you store your gin in the shadow of a vermouth bottle. Devotees are also known to pass the cap of the vermouth bottle quickly over the gin. The least plausible, but perhaps most amusing, tactic is to place a photograph of the man who invented vermouth in front of the gin.

On an unfortunate note, many people call almost anything in a Martini glass a Martini. Interlopers may share its name but not its glory. Other Martini variations that are not based on the classic gin cocktail will be found under the Vodkatini.

Flavor Affinities: Carpaccio of paper-thin sliced tenderloin, peppery cheese sticks with garlic, raw oysters, smoked salmon, or medallions of cold roast beef—the Martini offers a range of food possibilities as great as its mystique. If you are of the "less-is-more" school, you may want to forgo food entirely. In the words of Johnny Carson,

"Happiness is finding two olives in your Martini when you are hungry."

Recipes:

Martini:
3 ounces gin
Dry vermouth
Green olives or twist of lemon peel

Depending on your taste, mix 5 to 8 parts gin to 1 part vermouth for a dry Martini. Use less vermouth for a drier Martini. Stir in a pitcher half filled with ice, or shake with ice; then strain into a chilled cocktail glass. Garnish with green olives or lemon peel. A "bone-dry" Martini, also known as "pass the bottle," contains no vermouth whatsoever.

Variations:

The James Bond Martini, aka the Vesper (from Casino Royale):
3 ounces Gordon's gin
1 ounce vodka
¹/₂ ounce Kina Lillet
Green olives or twist of lemon peel

Shake the gin, vodka, and Lillet with ice; then strain into a chilled cocktail glass. Garnish with green olives or lemon peel.

The Gibson:

The Gibson is made exactly like the Martini, but a

small cocktail onion is substituted for the olive. A number of stories exist regarding its origin, but the consensus is that it was named for the illustrator Charles Dana Gibson, creator of the era's paradigm of female beauty, the Gibson Girl. Gibson and his cronies would often take a break from work and visit the Player's Club for a few drinks. While journalists may feel inspired after a drink or two, an artist needs an absolutely steady hand. Gibson furtively asked the bartender, Charlie Connolly, to give him pure ice water. The drink was distinguished by a silver-skinned cocktail onion. Patrons soon began ordering their Martinis with onions and calling them Gibsons to honor the inventor. Double onions were also ordered, paying homage to certain physical assets of the Gibson Girl.

Astoria:

Add a dash of bitters.

Blue Martini:

Substitute blue curaçao for the vermouth, and garnish with a maraschino cherry.

Cajun Martini:

Noted chef Paul Prudhomme invented this drink by infusing a cut-up jalapeño pepper in a bottle of gin for half a day. The spicy liquor replaces the ordinary gin. Garnish with a slice of green tomato or pickled jalapeño. Vodka may be substituted for the gin.

Dirty Martini:

Add a splash of olive brine, and garnish with a green olive.

Fino Martini:

Substitute fino sherry for the vermouth.

Knickerbocker Martini:

Substitute equal parts sweet and dry vermouth for the dry vermouth, and add a dash of bitters.

Montgomery:

Named for a British general who would not go into battle unless his troops outnumbered the opposition 25 to 1, this Martini uses the same proportion of gin to vermouth.

Naked Martini:

Omit the vermouth. After shaking, turn in the direction of France, bow, and pour.

Odyssey:

Mix Magellan French gin, Bossiere Italian vermouth, and a Greek cracked olive in brine.

Sakétini:

Substitute 1 ounce sake for the vermouth.

Silver Bullet:
Substitute Scotch for the vermouth.

63a–d.

MARY PICKFORD

General
Description:

The Mary Pickford is one of a variety of cocktails named for film luminaries. Movie stars have celebrated the merits of the cocktail as well as lamented its abuses. Ginger Rogers and Fred Astaire helped to immortalize the cocktail. The first words Greta Garbo uttered on screen were "Gimme a whiskey, ginger ale on the side, and don't be stingy, baby." Asked about how she was mixed up in a delicate situation, Mae West replied, "Like an olive in a dry Martini." These celebrities all have cocktails named after them. Thinking about those who played alcoholics in movies, however, there is no Ray Milland, Jack Lemmon, or Nicolas Cage, which shows that it pays to be respectful to your cocktail on screen.

Like sandwiches, drinks have been regularly baptized for stars, and the Mary Pickford, named for the early motion picture icon, is one of the earliest. It was so popular in its time that Douglas Fairbanks, who later married Pickford, asked a bartender in Cuba to name a cocktail after him. The bartender did. Wouldn't you? Most of the stars have faded into history, and so have their drinks. Presented here are a few dusty relics.

Purchase:	The classic bars that were home to the Mary Pickford and other celebrity drinks have been relegated to the museum of memory, so you will want to try mixing these cocktails at home.
Areas and Time of Occurrence: ☾	Rent a few DVDs of films from the bygone days and start mixing. *Sunset Boulevard* would be a good choice, but *Harvey*, the *Thin Man* series, or any W. C. Fields film would qualify. Fields claimed that he never drank anything stronger than gin before breakfast; take his advice and experiment with these curiosities at cocktail hour. Fields was said to have kept $50,000 worth of liquor in his attic after Prohibition. When George Burns asked why, Fields replied, "You never know if it's going to come back."
Season: ❀ ☼ ❀ ❄	Although there is no time like the present, you may want to sample a Mary Pickford after a lost weekend, while leaving Las Vegas, or during the days of wine and roses.
Flavor Affinities:	You could order Sid's Caesar Salad or the Richard Simmons Tropical Fruit Salad from the Stage Deli in New York.
Recipes:	***Mary Pickford:*** **1 ounce light rum** **1 ounce unsweetened pineapple juice** **1/4 teaspoon grenadine**

¹/₄ **teaspoon maraschino liqueur**
Maraschino cherry

Shake the rum, pineapple juice, grenadine, and maraschino liqueur with ice; then strain into a chilled cocktail glass. Garnish with a maraschino cherry.

Douglas Fairbanks:
1¹/₂ ounces gin
1 ounce apricot brandy or sweet vermouth
¹/₂ ounce fresh lime juice
Twist of lemon peel

Shake the gin, brandy, and lime juice with ice; then strain into a chilled cocktail glass. Garnish with lemon peel.

Garbo Gargle Cocktail:
1 ounce brandy
¹/₄ ounce fresh orange juice
¹/₄ ounce grenadine
¹/₄ ounce dry vermouth
Dash of crème de menthe
Dash of port wine

Shake the brandy, orange juice, grenadine, vermouth, and crème de menthe with ice; then strain into a chilled cocktail glass. Float the port on top.

Mae West:
Yolk of 1 egg
1 teaspoon superfine sugar
3 ounces brandy
Cayenne pepper

Shake the egg, sugar, and brandy very well with ice; then strain into a chilled cocktail glass. Dust with cayenne pepper.

---

64. **MINT JULEP**

General
Description:

The world-renowned Mint Julep is a mixture of mint, sugar, and bourbon, but some historians argue that the first juleps may have been made with common brandy. If Freud is more talked about than read, the Mint Julep is more read about than drunk. One survey revealed that while 70 percent of Americans not from the South had never tasted a Mint Julep, 73 percent of Southerners had never had one either. Champions of the Julep protest that the drink stirred up by the vat-full on Kentucky Derby Day is a pale horse to the spirited classic. Add to this that Bourbon County was originally owned by Virginia, also claiming the drink's invention, and you have a greater muddle than the mint in the bottom of the glass. I should mention that muddling mint is considered as abhorrent by some as it is extolled by others and that Maryland,

Pennsylvania, and Mississippi all also say they were home to the first Mint Julep.

Historically, the root of the Julep is not Southern or American, but Arabic—*julab* means "rosewater"— and doctors called any beverage that disguised the taste of medicine a "julep." Prior to the Civil War, brandy or whiskey was common in a julep, but the poverty of the South after the war gave rise to the use of less-expensive bourbon. As to the proper proportions, method of mixing, and who originated the cocktail, William Grimes in *Straight Up or On the Rocks* states: "If the mark of a great cocktail is the number of arguments it can provoke and the number of unbreakable rules it generates, the Mint Julep may be America's preeminent classic, edging out the Martini in a photo finish."

Purchase:	Purists would have it that purchasing a Mint Julep at the Kentucky Derby is like going to New York City in an "I ♥ New York" T-shirt. This is clearly one cocktail that deserves to be made at home.
Areas and Time of Occurrence:	Without dishonoring the tradition of the Kentucky Derby, the subtle complexity of a well-made Mint Julep is best savored on a country porch or veranda far from the madding crowd. Juleps, tempered by polite conversation and the soft chirping of birds, were created with late afternoon in mind.

Season:
A refreshing Mint Julep should be sipped in the summertime, when the living is easy. That's what Daisy in *The Great Gatsby* would recommend.

Preparation:
To muddle or not to muddle, that is the question that could result in fisticuffs. Francis Parkinson Keyes recalled the last words of a Virginia gentleman: "Never insult a woman, never bring a horse into the house, and never crush the mint in a julep." Whether or not you decide to crush your mint, make certain that it is fresh. And do leave the horse outdoors.

Flavor Affinities:
Despite the unseemly pairing of hot dogs with Mint Juleps at the Kentucky Derby, forgo the tube steak for applewood-smoked bacon bites or crispy fried oysters.

Recipe:
Mint Julep:
3 sprigs fresh mint
1 teaspoon water
1 teaspoon superfine sugar
2 ounces bourbon

Muddle 2 mint sprigs, the water, and the sugar in a highball or collins glass or a silver julep cup. Fill the glass with crushed ice, and pour in the bourbon. Garnish with the remaining mint sprig.

Variation:
Brandy Julep:
Omit the mint sprig garnish. Substitute brandy for

the bourbon, and garnish with a slice of orange and a
maraschino cherry.

65.   **MOJITO**

General
Description:
*Something of a **Mint Julep** made with rum, the Mojito
is always muddled with fresh mint leaves.* Ernest
Hemingway drained **Daiquiris** at Havana's La
Floridita, but he quaffed his Mojitos at La Bodeguita
del Medio—or so says the sign at La Bodeguita.
There is no substantial evidence, however, that Papa
ever bellied up to that bar, but he was certain to have
nibbled a few of these coolers in his time. La
Bodeguita did manage to take this plebeian drink
from the hands of the farmers and working class and
place it in those of the well-heeled. These efforts paid
off, and the Mojito became such a Cuban standard
during the 1930s and 1940s that it earned such
celebrity adherents as Errol Flynn, Nat King Cole,
and Lou Costello. The cocktail is enjoying a full-scale
revival today. The drink is so crisp and smooth that
you may be wondering who's on first if you don't
keep score of how many you are socking away.

Purchase:
The Mojito is still conspicuously absent from many
modern bartender's manuals, but it is rapidly catching
on as the drink of the moment. Try it at home, and it
will instantly become part of your repertoire.

Areas and Time of Occurrence:	The silver rum used in making a true Mojito is hard to come by outside Cuba, so the cocktail is a worthy excuse to visit Havana. Otherwise, sip this tall drink in the shade of a palm tree on a lazy afternoon. Parched and perched in front of an air conditioner on a sweltering day will also do.
Season:	If rum is your favorite potation, the Mojito may become your favorite summertime refresher.
Preparation:	If you know how to make a Mint Julep—and you should—you can muddle up a Mojito. Muddle the entire mint sprig to release the juice from the stem, and add a generous squeeze of lime right before serving. La Bodeguita bartender Jorge Lorenzo Viqueira Lee advises that you follow the ingredient proportions religiously to achieve the harmony of flavors that makes a perfect Mojito. You may also add a dash of bitters.
Flavor Affinities:	Tapas are ideal companions for this summer drink, but you can also go whole hog here and serve an entire roast pig.
Recipe:	***Mojito:*** **3 small sprigs fresh mint** **1 teaspoon superfine sugar** **1¹/₂ ounces light rum** **2 ounces cold club soda**

Muddle 2 mint sprigs with the sugar in a mixing glass. Add the rum, and shake with ice. Strain into a collins or highball glass; then top with the soda, and garnish with the remaining mint sprig.

66.   **MONKEY GLAND**

General
Description:

The Monkey Gland is a gin-based cocktail blended with orange juice and enlivened by grenadine and Pernod. Few classic cocktails of such appealing character have such odious names. Harry MacElhone, owner of Harry's New York Bar in Paris, is credited with mixing the first Monkey Gland in the 1920s. The sonorous sobriquet was inspired by the work of Serge Voronoff, a Russian who experimented with the sexual organs of monkeys for rejuvenation. The verdict is not in on the procedures with the naughty bits of monkeys, but the bygone fashionable drink is a reliable rejuvenator.

Purchase:

Order a Monkey Gland by its ingredients rather than its name. Older bartenders may have a flash of recognition, but younger ones will be clueless. Tell them it's something you've been monkeying around with.

Areas and Time
of Occurrence:

The more traditional, well-stocked bars and cocktail lounges are the best venues to grab a Monkey Gland. If you need an eye-opening drink after work, a stimulant before dinner, or a reminder of the good old days of simian testicular research, the Monkey Gland is the unqualified answer.

Season:

If the restorative powers of a Monkey Gland are genuine—only some experiment and observation should bear this out—it could become a timeless elixir.

Preparation:

The original recipe for the Monkey Gland called for anisette, but both Pernod and Bénédictine have become common substitutions. Consummate New York bartender Dale DeGroff, who uses the latter, also adds a flamed orange peel (page 21).

Flavor Affinities:

Your guests may not have an appetite after learning the name of this cocktail, but when they come around, serve a wedge of extra-sharp cheddar with crackers or a simple bowl of party mix.

Recipe:

Monkey Gland:
2 ounces gin
1¹/₂ ounces fresh orange juice
2 dashes of grenadine
2 dashes of Pernod or Bénédictine
Twist of orange peel

Shake the gin, orange juice, grenadine, and Pernod very well with ice; then strain into a chilled cocktail glass. Garnish with orange peel.

67. **MOSCOW MULE**

General
Description:

The Moscow Mule is a vodka-based cocktail with the unusual addition of ginger beer. Vodka was still relatively unknown outside Russia and Central Europe in the years following World War II. Heublein president John Martin had recently purchased the Smirnoff name and recipe for his American company, and he was out to promote his new product. As the story goes, Martin stopped off for dinner and drinks at the Cock 'n' Bull on Sunset Strip, where his friend, owner Jack Morgan, was struggling to sell his homemade ginger beer. Add to the mix another friend who had inherited a large collection of copper mugs—and shake with a massive dose of publicity and a wedge of lime—and you have the Moscow Mule. In one of the most successful marketing ploys in tippling history, Martin combined three seemingly hopeless endeavors into one of the most popular cocktails of the 1950s and early 1960s. He even got stars like Woody Allen to promote his concoction. But as popular as it was, the Moscow Mule has now entered the "endangered species list" and is rarely seen outside of vintage ads in old issues of *Playboy* magazine.

Purchase:

Be prepared to face stares of curiosity if you ask a young bartender to make you a Moscow Mule. This refreshing potion is so easy to make that it is the perfect drink to concoct at home.

Areas and Time of Occurrence:	The Moscow Mule has been relegated to the Museum of Memory, along with Nehru jackets, go-go boots, and Trini Lopez records, but there is no reason why you can't lie back in a hammock on a summer afternoon with a good book and a cool Mule.
Season:	With marketing as its modus operandi, the Moscow Mule has been touted as a summer drink as well as a cool vodka libation with a slow ginger burn that warms the blood on cold winter nights.
Preparation:	Substituting ginger ale for ginger beer in a Moscow Mule is tantamount to using 7-Up for a Cuba Libre. The authentic way to drink a Moscow Mule is in the original copper cup, with an embossed kicking mule on one side.
Flavor Affinities:	Select cheese logs, pigs-in-a-blanket, bologna boats, and the like.
Recipe:	***Moscow Mule:*** **1¹/₂ ounces vodka** **Wedge of lime** **Cold ginger beer**

Pour the vodka into a copper mug or an iced glass. Squeeze the lime over the vodka, and drop the wedge into the mug. Fill the glass with the ginger beer.

Variation:

Mobile Mule:

Substitute 2 ounces light rum for the the vodka.

68. **NEGRONI**

General
Description:

Even with equal parts Campari, gin, and vermouth, the bitterness of a Negroni firmly establishes the drink as a Campari-based cocktail. No one is undecided about a Negroni. This Italian big brother to the **Americano** and distant cousin to the **Martini** is so bitter that its dissenters swear it should be stored in the medicine chest. Its fanatical adherents bask in its ruddy glow and tongue-tingling taste. Some contend that this classic cocktail dates back to Florence in the 1920s, when the flamboyant count—and noted tippler—Camillo Negroni asked for a splash of gin added to his Americano. Others say that the drink, mixed with vodka or gin, has been around as long as the Americano. The Campari company, itself unsure of the origin, eventually decided that the drink should be called a Negroni to avoid confusion with all the other Campari cocktails.

Purchase:

As with the Americano, you are more likely to find this drink at continental cafés and restaurants. If you favor the assertive bite of Campari, you can easily put the color back in your cheeks by mixing it at home.

<table>
<tr><td>Areas and Time
of Occurrence:
</td><td>Order a Negroni when you want an Americano with a wallop to it. Of course, if you don't want an Americano to begin with, stick with a Martini, but next time you are sitting in a trattoria or outdoor café feeling adventurous, give the Negroni a try. Any culture that gave the world the Renaissance, spaghetti carbonara, and Sophia Loren at least deserves a shot.</td></tr>
</table>

Season:

A tart Negroni bites back at the chill of cool weather and embraces the heat of summer.

Preparation:

For a longer drink, serve a Negroni with a splash of soda. The cocktail may also be shaken and poured straight up in a cocktail glass.

Flavor
Affinities:

An antipasti platter with an array of salty cold cuts, marinated vegetables, and hard cheeses is a crowning touch to the complex body of a Negroni.

Recipe:

Negroni:
1 ounce gin
1 ounce sweet vermouth
1 ounce Campari
Slice of orange

Pour the gin, vermouth, and Campari into a chilled old-fashioned glass over ice; then garnish with a slice of orange.

Variation: ***Dry Negroni:***

Substitute dry vermouth for the sweet vermouth.

69.   **OLD FASHIONED**

General
Description: *One of America's oldest cocktails, the Old Fashioned is*
short for "old fashioned whiskey cocktail." Rye whiskey
is the base for this drink, which is rounded out by the
addition of fruit. An Old Fashioned is, well, old-
fashioned—but in an entirely laudable way. Its notoriety
was so widespread that a particular glass was named for
it. Practically everyone has heard of this tried-and-true
classic cocktail that dates back to the 1880s, but the
general assumption is that the Old Fashioned is an
innocuous fruity mélange with the kick of a glazed
doughnut. While definitely fruity by nature, the drink
is hardly a pushover. On the contrary, the Old
Fashioned is built on a very solid helping of whiskey,
and three of these drinks will show you who's boss—
the Old Fashioned. Which whiskey should be used is
cause for fierce debate. The drink was first poured at
the Pendennis Club in Kentucky, but it is not clear
whether rye or bourbon was the spirit of choice. In
Cole Porter's "Make It Another Old Fashioned Please,"
he says rye—and he ought to know.

Another unremitting controversy is whether to
muddle the fruit or leave it whole. Yet another point
of discussion is what form of sugar to use: a cube,

granulated, or simple syrup. Whatever your decision, for a consummate Old Fashioned, the velvety texture of the fruit should harmonize with the pungency of the whiskey. One anonymous wag has said, "The Old Fashioned, with its layered taste, is an open invitation for both the whiskey lover and the froufrou-cocktail drinker. It's frilly but disciplined: Cocktail compadres compare it to a good old-fashioned spanking."

Purchase:

The Old Fashioned, in its various incarnations, is still a bar standard. If you go to a different bar every day for a month, you may taste as many different Old Fashioneds. The home bartender should certainly experiment with this cocktail.

Areas and Time of Occurrence:

🌙

The Old Fashioned finds itself in the manicured hands of the pretheater crowd at Sardi's in New York as well as in the gnarly mitts of truckers stopping for a nightcap at a roadhouse along Route 66. If you order it at the Bull 'n' Finch Pub—the original Cheers—in Boston, it will be made with bourbon.

Season:

Some disciples of the Old Fashioned will sip this libation whenever the mood strikes them. But there is something about an Old Fashioned, with its festive cherry and orange, that gives it a holiday-season flair.

Preparation:

Rye is a rarity these days, so even the purist should not feel guilty about using bourbon. Old Fashioneds can also be made with blended whiskey or brandy.

Flavor
Affinities:
Pair nostalgic foods with the venerable Old Fashioned. Deviled mushrooms, cold tongue, and parslied onion sandwiches will all rekindle memories, even if they belong to your grandparents.

Recipe:
Classic Old Fashioned:
2 maraschino cherries and 2 slices of orange
1 teaspoon sugar or 1 small sugar cube
1 or 2 dashes of Angostura bitters
1 teaspoon water
2 ounces rye or bourbon whiskey

Muddle 1 cherry, 1 orange slice, and the sugar, bitters, and water in a chilled old-fashioned glass. Remove the orange rind. Add the whiskey and ice; then stir. Garnish with a maraschino cherry and an orange slice.

70. **ORANGE BLOSSOM**

General
Description:
Equal parts gin and orange juice, with a touch of sugar, make up the Orange Blossom. Although upon first glance one might believe that the Orange Blossom is a simple variation on a **Screwdriver**, the Orange Blossom's pedigree predates the latter by many years and should be considered a parent to the vodka version. The

Orange Blossom harks back to Prohibition, when the harshness of homemade gin needed to be diluted to make it palatable. H. L. Mencken praised it as one of the few drinks one could depend upon, but in 1934 *Esquire* magazine called it one of the ten worst cocktails of the 1930s. There is just no pleasing everyone. Because much of the spirits that were drunk during the unfortunate era of the Noble Experiment were distilled in the Adirondack Mountains, the cocktail was nicknamed the Adirondack Special. With oranges as a chief ingredient, it also came to be known as the Florida.

Purchase:

Not all bars will know the name of this drink, so it may be necessary to order by ingredients. It is also ridiculously simple to make at home.

Areas and Time of Occurrence:

The Orange Blossom may have been born amid the sawdust and stale liquor of the speakeasy, but it has evolved into an ideal summertime thirst quencher. Next time you are about to have a Screwdriver with brunch, try one of these instead.

Season:

As soon as the cool days are behind you, Orange Blossom time begins.

Preparation:

Common granulated sugar was most likely used during Prohibition, but the Orange Blossom has been refined with simple syrup and even Cointreau.

Flavor
Affinities:
Orange Blossoms go remarkably well with grilled faji-
tas or guacamole and chips.

Recipe:
Orange Blossom:
1¹/₂ ounces gin
1¹/₂ ounces fresh orange juice
1 teaspoon superfine sugar or simple syrup
Slice of orange

Pour the gin, orange juice, and sugar into a cold old-
fashioned glass over ice, then garnish with a slice of
orange. Alternatively, shake with ice, then strain into
a chilled cocktail glass and garnish with a flamed
orange peel (page 21).

71.

PARIS IS BURNING

General
Description:
*The preparation of a Paris Is Burning, which requires
careful heating, is as vital to the cocktail as its essential
ingredients of cognac and Chambord.* According to
Gary and Mardee Regan in their book *New Classic
Cocktails,* an unknown bartender at Salty's on Alki, in
Seattle, produced the first version of this cocktail for
an executive on the board of the company that owned
Chambord liqueur. Brandy and cognac are often
warmed by the hands or a slight flame to release the
heady aroma, and the bartender followed this princi-
ple by heating the cocktail with a cappuccino

machine. The executive was so thrilled with it that Chambord introduced it with the question "Is Paris Burning?" in one of its marketing brochures. This new-wave cocktail, with its casual elegance, is rapidly catching on, and it may well find its way into the classic repertory. The name is a reference to heat generated by the French ingredients and has no relation to any heat generated by similarly named human celebrities of esteemed hotel lineage.

Purchase:

A Paris Is Burning is best heated by steam from a cappuccino machine. Upscale bars that have access to one would be the spot to order this drink, but it takes little effort to prepare at home, too.

Areas and Time of Occurrence:

🌙

Nights in Seattle can be rainy and bitingly cold. It's easy to see how the Paris Is Burning was created there. But this postprandial will take the chill out of any frosty night.

Season:

❄ ❅

Mix a Paris Is Burning any evening when the chill lingers in your hands and an extra sweater just seems like dead weight.

Preparation:

Paris Is Burning should be warm, but absolutely not hot. Bartenders who have access to cappuccino machines heat the brandy with the steam from the machine, but an old-fashioned brandy warmer or a saucepan on the stovetop will also do. The Regans suggest using a microwave oven for 20 seconds.

Flavor
Affinities:

Finger foods like onion tartlets would fare well if you serve this cocktail on its own, but crêpes suzettes or an assortment of chocolate truffles would make for a felicitous culmination to the end of a long day.

Recipe:

Paris Is Burning:
2 ounces cognac
¹/₂ ounce Chambord or raspberry-flavored liqueur

Stir the cognac and Chambord in a small saucepan over low heat until the liquid is warm to the touch, about 40 seconds. Pour into a large brandy snifter.

72a–c.

PICK-ME-UPS

General
Description:

A Pick-Me-Up is any number of recipes concocted at times to revive one's mood but more often to soften the pain of overindulgence. Anyone who has experienced the ill effects of one too many would agree with Robert Benchley that "the only cure for a hangover is death." Dean Martin's cure was not as drastic: "Stay drunk." Some blends are so loathsome that they are merely the variation on the concept that if you poke yourself in the eye, you will forget about your stubbed toe. The **Bloody Mary** is considered by many to be the universal panacea for this dismal state, but another cocktail first served at the Ritz Bar in Paris in the 1920s has perhaps the most stimulating name of any of these cure-alls: the Corpse Reviver. Harry Craddock, in *The Savoy Cocktail Book*, gave this advice for his Corpse Reviver #1: "to be taken before 11 A.M., or whenever steam and energy are needed." For his Corpse Reviver #2, he warned: "Four of these taken in straight succession will unrevive the corpse again." Blitzed, blotto, buttered—there may be as many synonyms for drunk as there are cocktails, but there is only one hangover.

Purchase: If you have overdone it a bit, it is very likely you will not be in the mood to mix a Pick-Me-Up yourself. Luckily, there will always be a benevolent and understanding bartender—or a wiseass who did not overdo it—who will be happy to accommodate you.

Areas and Time of Occurrence: The best time for a Pick-Me-Up is late morning—the later, the better.

Season: To every season there is a purpose, and the purpose is quite clear here.

Preparation: There is no guarantee that any of these recipes will work for you, so bear in mind that practicing moderation is better than the cure. Drink plenty of water the night before to prevent dehydration. Eating fatty, high-protein foods may slow the alcohol absorption. Take two tacos and call us in the morning.

Flavor Affinities:	Brunch fare, and particularly eggs, bacon, and toast, are candidates for Pick-Me-Up pairings.
Recipes:	***Savoy Corpse Reviver:***

Savoy Corpse Reviver:
1 ounce Fernet Branca
1 ounce brandy
1 ounce white crème de menthe

 Shake all ingredients with ice; then strain into a chilled cocktail glass.

Corpse Reviver 2:
1 ounce gin
$^1/_2$ ounce Lillet
$^1/_2$ ounce Cointreau
$^1/_2$ ounce Pernod or anise-flavored liqueur
$^3/_4$ ounce fresh lemon juice

Shake all ingredients with ice; then strain into a chilled cocktail glass.

Prairie Oyster:
1 whole egg
1 ounce vodka
2 dashes of vinegar
1 teaspoon Worcestershire sauce
1 teaspoon ketchup
2 dashes of Tabasco sauce
Pinch of salt and pepper

Carefully crack the egg into an old-fashioned glass, taking care not to break the yolk. Add the remaining ingredients, and drink in one gulp.

73. **PIMM'S CUP**

General
Description:

Pimm's No. 1 is a gin-based potation made in England from dry gin, liqueur, fruit juices, and spices. Served with lemon soda or ginger ale, it becomes a Pimm's Cup. Pimm's No. 1 was created in the mid-eighteenth century by English oyster bar owner James Pimm. The recipe is still a secret; supposedly, only six people know exactly how it is made. It has a dark, golden brown color, a medium body, and a taste of quinine, citrus fruits, and spice. Its low alcohol content of only 25 percent has made Pimm's a drink to have when you are having more than one. As was customary at the time, Pimm served the cocktail in tankards— hence the name "Pimm's Cup." The rage for this relative of the Sling became so great that Pimm mass-produced and bottled it along with Pimm's 2, 3, 4, 5, and 6: whiskey, brandy, rum, rye, and vodka, respectively. Detractors have likened the earthy mixture to liquid dirt mellowed by iodine, but the Pimm's Cup is still the traditional drink of Wimbledon, with visitors to the matches consuming some forty thousand pints a year. The addition of a cucumber slice gives the drink some truck as a health food. Some.

| Purchase: | English-style pubs will be happy to make you an authentic Pimm's Cup; try one before you decide to make this unique cocktail at home. |

Areas and Time of Occurrence: The **Mint Julep** may be the nonofficial drink of the Kentucky Derby, but the Pimm's Cup is the official drink of Wimbledon. If you cannot make it to the matches, sip the drink while watching them on TV. Low as it is in alcohol, it's also a much-needed companion to your first cricket match.

Season: For those who enjoy it, the Pimm's Cup is as fresh as the first days of spring, and a delightful way to welcome the new season.

Preparation: The English traditionally mix their Pimm's No. 1 with "lemonade," which is akin to 7-Up or Sprite. Abroad, the Pimm's is blended with any number of mixers, ginger ale being a favorite with many bartenders.

Flavor Affinities: The Pimm's Cup couples with savory foods such as Cornish pasties, spiced shrimp balls, or curried eggs.

Recipe: *Pimm's Cup:*
2 ounces Pimm's No. 1
7-Up, lemon-lime soda, or ginger ale
Slice of lemon
Slice of cucumber

Pour the Pimm's and 7-Up in a chilled highball glass or metal cup over ice. Squeeze a slice of lemon well as you drop it in the glass; then stir gently, and garnish with a cucumber slice.

74.   **PIÑA COLADA**

General Description:

The Piña Colada cocktail consists of rum, cream of coconut, and pineapple juice. Whereas the **Martini** has been esteemed as the king of cocktails, the Piña Colada, sadly, has been belittled as the jester—as anything so carefree and fun loving is bound to be. It didn't help when the breezy "Piña Colada Song" became as much a lounge staple as swizzle sticks. (The Rupert Holmes tune is actually titled "Escape.") Rum and pineapple juice have always been natural partners, but cream of coconut, introduced in 1952, would make for an indivisible ménage à trois. Ramon Manchito Marrero Pérez was tending bar at the Caribe Hilton when he was introduced to the product Coco Lopez, and the Piña Colada, translated as "squeezed pineapple," was born. A sign at La Barra in San Juan's Old City has a different claim: In 1963, the Piña Colada was created there by Don Ramón Portas Migot. That both claimants have four names might indicate a tie, but most authorities credit Pérez.

Purchase:

Almost every seaside resort features the Piña Colada,

but steer clear of bars that premix the drink. Cream of coconut is widely available, which makes this an easy home-blender cooler.

Areas and Time of Occurrence:

If there ever was a "boat drink," it is the Piña Colada. Mixed with crushed ice, the Piña Colada requires very little water in it, but oceans around it. The versatile Piña Colada is readily adapted to afternoon volleyball on the beach, early evenings spent watching the tide roll out, or a night of dancing to Perez Prado or Martin Denny.

Season:

Summer, summer, and summer is when to sip a Piña Colada.

Preparation:

A Piña Colada can be made a bit more pungent by using a mix of light and dark rum. For a slightly pulpier drink, substitute 2 ounces crushed pineapple for 2 ounces pineapple juice. Do not mistake coconut milk for cream of coconut.

Flavor Affinities:

Fresh seafood appetizers or sushi with wasabi go beautifully with a frosty Piña Colada, and Chinese appetizers, such as scallion pancakes or spring rolls with ginger dipping sauce, provide a snappy contrast.

Recipe:

Piña Colada:
2 ounces light rum
2 ounces cream of coconut

1 ounce heavy cream
4 ounces unsweetened pineapple juice
Slice of pineapple and a maraschino cherry

Place the rum, cream of coconut, heavy cream, and pineapple juice in a blender, and blend for a few seconds. Add ¹/2 cup crushed ice, and blend for another 15 seconds, or until smooth. Pour into an exotic glass of your choice. Garnish with a pineapple slice and a maraschino cherry.

Variations: **Chi Chi:**
Substitute vodka for the rum.

Banana Colada:
Peel, slice, and freeze 3 bananas; then add them to the blender in place of the ice.

75a–b. **PINK LADY**

General
Description:

Grenadine adds the pink to a Pink Lady, and gin does the rest. The Pink Lady was another Prohibition drink created more out of necessity than from a dedication to the art of mixology. It has been noted that Prohibition gin could be very nasty. To tame a flavor that could be likened to a glass of live bumble bees, drinkers experimented with just about anything on hand. The Pink Lady spawned a bevy of grenadine "pink" cocktails in the 1930s; *The Savoy Cocktail Book* lists five. With the end of prohibition, the Pink Lady's popularity began to fade. The drink even had the dubious honor of making *Esquire* magazine's notorious ten worst cocktails list. Do not confuse this plucky Pink Lady with another present-day cocktail of the same name. The latter is made with vodka, vermouth, and strawberry milk shake.

Purchase: While most bartenders will have heard of a Pink Lady, few will know how to make it. But that will not stop them from trying.

Areas and Time of Occurrence: The place and time for endangered drinks like the Pink Lady have all but disappeared. If you were to host a period-piece murder-mystery party, the Pink Lady would fit right in with the arm-length white gloves, spats, and foot-long cigarette holders.

Season: The addition of an egg white would make the summery Pink Lady a cooler-weather drink.

Preparation: Some recipes make the Pink Lady even smoother by adding more heavy cream. Lemon juice or simple syrup may also be added.

Flavor Affinities: All savory appetizers suit the Pink Lady, but you may want shrimp toast or Welsh rarebit on the menu.

Recipe: ***Pink Lady:***
              2 ounces gin
              1 teaspoon grenadine
              1 egg white (optional)
              ¹/₂ ounce heavy cream

 Shake all ingredients vigorously with ice until frothy;
then strain into a chilled cocktail glass.

Variations: ***Pink Panther:***
 Substitute 1 ounce vodka and 1 ounce amaretto for
the gin, and omit the egg.

Pink Rose:
 Substitute light cream for the heavy cream, and add a
dash of fresh lemon juice.

76a–f. 🔘   ## POUSSE CAFÉ

General   *Also called a rainbow cordial, the Pousse Café is an*
Description: *after-dinner drink composed of several colored liqueurs*
              skillfully poured into a narrow, straight cordial glass.
              Because of their differing weights and densities, the indi-
              vidual layers of ingredients remain distinct. Derived
              from the French for "pushes coffee," the Pousse Café
              is served with or after coffee. Like a splendid, multi-
              colored peacock, the Pousse Café elicits admiration.
              The carefully layered spirits may be as subtle as the

striations in a seashell or as brash as the colors of a national flag. For those who favor liqueurs, it is a marvel to behold and to drink, because each layer is meant to complement the next, and the cocktail should be sipped slowly to savor each flavor. These libations became quite popular during Prohibition and the Jazz Age, and their individual names, reflecting their contents, range from the subtle to the explicit.

The Pousse Café also has its detractors. Thomas Mario, in *Playboy's Host and Bar Book*, asserts: "This showy little drink is one of the oldest bits of nonsense known to bartenders—and, needless to say, the number of drinkers who never stop loving nonsense is greater than ever." Just as corsets have gone out of fashion, one might have expected that so, too, would the Pousse Café. Corsets have made a return, however, and the Pousse Café is more popular than ever, albeit under the less urbane title of **Shooter**.

Purchase:	The Pousse Café demands a variety of liqueurs for its myriad combinations and a skilled hand for pouring.
Areas and Time of Occurrence:	Once a denizen of the drawing room, today the Pousse Café is more likely to be found among the new wave of young drinkers in swingers bars or chic dance clubs. It is definitely a late-night drink. If it is ever seen during the daylight hours, it is in the nimble hands of a young aficionado attempting to perfect his or her pouring technique.

Season:

There is a festive Pousse Café for each season as well as for seasons yet to be discovered.

Preparation:

Happily, there is actually a glass called a Pousse Café. Sadly, it is difficult to find. It resembles a pony glass but flares out slightly at the top. You will need to select a recipe of your choice, or you may experiment with the density chart of liqueurs below. As a rule of thumb, the higher the alcohol content, the lower the density. Pour your heaviest liquid first, and then place the bowl of a bar spoon or teaspoon upside down into the glass against the edge. Slowly pour the next heaviest liqueur over the back of the spoon, and continue with each liqueur, ending with the lightest. Stand back and wait for applause. See page 298 for a chart of different liqueurs from heaviest to lightest.

Flavor
Affinities:

Being an after-dinner and after-hours cocktail, the Pousse Café is better suited to lightly salted snacks or assorted bar munchies, but nothing greasy or heavy.

Recipes:

Note: There is no one Pousse Café recipe; rather, different flavor combinations have been experimented with based on various liquid densities to produce the layered effect. Layer equal parts of the ingredients in a pony glass exactly as they are listed.

ABC: Amaretto, Bailey's Irish Cream, and Cointreau.

Angel's Kiss: Crème de cacao, brandy, and light cream.

Angel's Tip (or Tit): White crème de cacao, maraschino liqueur, and light cream. Garnish with a maraschino cherry.

B-52: Kahlúa, Bailey's Irish cream, and Grand Marnier.

Chocolate-Covered Cherry: Grenadine, Kahlúa, and Bailey's Irish Cream.

Easter Egg: Chambord, Tia Maria, and light cream.

Mexican Flag: Grenadine, green crème de menthe, and tequila.

Slippery Nipple: Sambuca and Bailey's Irish Cream.

---

77. **PRESIDENTE**

General Description:

Light rum, vermouth, and grenadine are constants in the Presidente, but the fruit flavoring varies. Cuba may have secured its place in cocktail history by contributing the **Cuba Libre**, **Daiquiri**, and **Mojito** to the world, but during its heyday sparked by Prohibition, the island's bartenders created dozens of splendid drinks to sate the palates of the hordes of visiting tourists. The Presidente, or El Presidente, was named

for the now-forgotten president of Cuba, General
Carmen Menocal. Credit has been given to La
Floridita's famed bartender Constantino Ribailagua
for popularizing the Presidente, but other sources
point to the Vista Alegre as the first watering hole in
Havana to have served it. *The Savoy Cocktail Book* and
others call it the President. Although Herbert Hoover
described the cocktail hour as "the pause between the
errors and trials of the day and the hopes of the
night," and although Roosevelt's penchant for the
Dirty Martini is legend, the present era of seeming
presidential cocktail indifference would beg the case
for keeping the name El Presidente.

Purchase: Some bartenders will beam with pleasure when you
order this chestnut, while others will smile and rush
to their bartender's guide. Get out your best shaker
and mix this user-friendly drink at home.

Areas and Time
of Occurrence:

The Presidente is another cooling seaside or poolside
drink that will quench your thirst at any hour. Served
as a balmy apéritif, a Presidente sets the pace for a
casual friendly gathering over hors d'oeuvres.

Season: This cocktail is particularly welcome in an election year
when you need something authentic to inspire you.

Preparation: You may substitute half sweet and half dry vermouth
for a sweeter drink, and as is typical of drinks with

sweet vermouth, you would add a maraschino cherry to it. Light and dark rum may also be used. Some recipes call for pineapple juice. Ignore them.

Flavor
Affinities:

Light, breezy fare such as salmon, shrimp, or a salad of hearts of palm could be included in a spread of appetizers.

Recipe:

Presidente:
1¹/₂ ounces light rum
¹/₂ ounce dry vermouth
¹/₂ ounce Cointreau
¹/₂ ounce fresh lemon juice
Dash of grenadine
Twist of lemon peel

Shake the rum, vermouth, Cointreau, lemon juice, and grenadine with ice; then strain into a chilled cocktail glass. Garnish with lemon peel.

 78a–c.

PUNCHES

General
Description:

The word punch *is probably derived from the Hindi word* panch, *meaning "five," because of its five basic ingredients: citrus juice, water, spices, sugar, and arrack, which is fermented palm sap, rice, or molasses.* The ingredients today are almost limitless. Punches were staples at pubs, taverns, and inns during the eighteenth and nineteenth centuries. British actor David

Garrick and lexicographer Samuel Johnson tried to
outdo each other by concocting newer and stronger
punches, while George Washington was partial to the
legendary Fish House Punch, introduced in 1732 at
the Schuylkill Fishing Club in Philadelphia. Punches
eventually became familiar sights at any social gathering. Just as colleges all had their own mascots, Yale
Punch, Harvard Punch, and Columbia Punch were
formulated in the 1920s. Punches were in such
demand in the 1930s that *The Savoy Cocktail Book*
lists 15, and their popularity only increased, as can be
witnessed by the twenty recipes given in the 1971
Playboy's Host and Bar Book. It may just be time to
unwrap that punch bowl you have tucked away for
the next tag sale and start a tradition of your own.

Purchase:

Punches are time-consuming and should be made in
bulk, so few establishments offer them. Home is
where the hearth and punch bowl are.

Areas and Time
of Occurrence:

If you happen upon establishments that serve punches,
they will most likely be relics of a bygone era—as will
be the bartenders who know how to make them.
Cocktail hour has supplanted the punch bowl at weddings, but there are still occasions steeped in tradition
that will feature a magnificent cut-glass bowl handed
down from generation to generation. Genteel gatherings such as church socials and afternoon teas will also
feature punches as a mannerly way of getting slightly

tipsy. But most punches are made at home for after-noon or early evening get-togethers.

Season: Cold weather calls for a glass of warm punch. The very word *punch* conjures up wassail and eggnog, but summer fruit punches are just as plentiful as winter-time recipes, and they can be as refreshing as their counterparts can be comforting.

Preparation: Instead of adding ice cubes, you can freeze water in a plastic mixing bowl or a large decorative mold. Because they are made in large quantities, punches may need to be adjusted to your taste. Strong tea is also common to cold punches.

Flavor Affinities: Given their size, punches should be served at large parties where a number of appetizers and hors d'oeuvres—such as stuffed artichoke hearts, mini quiches, and crudités with dips—will be presented. For cooler-weather punches, serve platters of cold meats such as turkey or whole tenderloin with horse-radish sauce.

Recipes: ***Artillery Punch:***
(Serves 30)
1 quart strong black tea
1 quart rye or blended whiskey
1 (750 ml) bottle red wine
1 pint dark rum

¹/₂ pint brandy
2 ounces Bénédictine
1 pint fresh orange juice
¹/₂ pint fresh lemon juice
Twists of lemon peel for each glass

Pour the tea, whiskey, wine, rum, brandy, Bénédictine, orange juice, and lemon juice into a large bowl over a large disk of ice. Stir until blended, and refrigerate for 1 hour. Serve in chilled glasses, and garnish with lemon peel.

Eggnog:
(Serves 20)
12 eggs, separated
1 cup granulated sugar
8 ounces bourbon
8 ounces cognac
¹/₂ teaspoon salt
3 pints heavy cream
Freshly grated nutmeg

Beat the egg yolks and sugar in a large bowl until light in color, about 3 minutes. Slowly add the bourbon and cognac while beating at slow speed. Chill for 3 hours. Place the egg whites in a separate bowl, add the salt, and with clean beaters, beat a few minutes to form peaks. Set aside. In a clean, chilled bowl, whip the cream until stiff, using clean beaters. Fold the whipped cream into the yolk mixture. Fold the beaten egg whites into the cream-yolk mixture. Chill for 1 hour. Pour into a punch bowl, and sprinkle nutmeg on top. Serve in chilled mugs. For a thinner mixture, add 1 to 2 cups of milk.

Fish House Punch:
(Serves 20)
³/₄ cup superfine sugar
5 cups water
3 cups dark rum
3 cups fresh lemon juice
3 cups brandy or cognac
1 pint peach brandy
2 peaches, peeled and sliced

Pour the sugar, water, rum, lemon juice, brandy, and peach brandy into a large bowl over a large disk of ice. Stir until blended, and refrigerate for 1 hour. Add the peach slices to float, and serve in chilled glasses.

Planter's Punch Cocktail:
(Serves 1)
1¹/₂ ounces light rum
³/₄ ounce fresh lemon juice
Dash of fresh orange juice
Wedge of lemon

Shake the rum, lemon juice, and orange juice well with ice; then strain into a chilled cocktail glass. Garnish with a lemon wedge.

Tom and Jerry:
(Serves 4)
3 eggs, separated
3 tablespoons powdered sugar
$1/2$ teaspoon ground allspice
$1/2$ teaspoon ground cinnamon
$1/2$ teaspoon ground cloves
4 ounces brandy, lukewarm
4 ounces dark rum, lukewarm
Hot milk
Freshly grated nutmeg

In a large, clean bowl, beat the egg whites until stiff peaks form. In a separate bowl, beat the egg yolks until light in color; gradually beat in the sugar, allspice, cinnamon, and cloves. Fold the yolk mixture into the whites. Pour 2 tablespoons into four mugs each. Add 1 ounce brandy and 1 ounce dark rum to each mug. Fill with hot milk. Stir well, and dust with nutmeg.

79.   **ROB ROY**

General
Description:

The Rob Roy is a blend of Scotch and vermouth sharpened by a dash of Angostura bitters. SAT experts every-

where would agree that a **Martini** is to a **Vodka Martini** as a **Manhattan** is to a Rob Roy. A Manhattan is a blend of rye or bourbon and sweet vermouth, and the Rob Roy is a mixture of Scotch and sweet vermouth; the difference is as sharp as that between a yam and a Yukon Gold. Anyone familiar with the 1995 film *Rob Roy* knows the source for the name of this cocktail—Robert MacGregor, the Scottish Robin Hood. Of course, unless you're a Scottish history buff, if you heard someone order a Rob Roy before 1995 you may have been a bit puzzled. Although we do not know who christened the Rob Roy for that feisty Scottish hero, according to William Grimes in *Straight Up or On the Rocks*, the drink was named for a Broadway play based on Sir Walter Scott's 1817 novel *Rob Roy*. Just as feisty, the Rob Roy gives you a wealth of enjoyment; the only thing it may rob you of is your memory after one too many.

Purchase: Any bartender worth his kilt—or what's under it— will know how to make a Rob Roy. Less knowledgeable bartenders have been known to serve the nonalcoholic Roy Rogers instead. The Rob Roy is a must for the home bartender.

Areas and Time of Occurrence: If the Manhattan is Gershwin's "Rhapsody in Blue," the Rob Roy is Johnny Mercer and Harold Arlen's "One for My Baby" (and One More for the Road). The former evokes dancing at the Ritz, while the latter suggests a loosened tie and dangling cigarette. Try ordering a Rob Roy in place of a Manhattan, and see if you can tell the difference.

Season:

The Rob Roy is a drink for all seasons, but you may serve it straight up in the cooler months and over the rocks in summer.

Preparation:

Follow your instincts on whether to stir or shake, but as with the Manhattan, a Rob Roy doesn't lose much by not being served glacially cold. The classic Rob Roy is served with a maraschino cherry, but some shudder at this and substitute a twist of lemon peel.

Flavor Affinities:

Follow the same guiding principles as for a Manhattan. Cheese-stuffed mushrooms are a tasty option.

Recipe:

Rob Roy:
2¹/₂ ounces Scotch
1 ounce sweet vermouth
Dash of Angostura bitters
Maraschino cherry or twist of lemon peel

Shake the Scotch, vermouth, and bitters with ice; then strain into a chilled cocktail glass. Garnish with a maraschino cherry or lemon peel.

Variations:

Dry Rob Roy:
Substitute dry vermouth for the sweet vermouth.

Perfect Rob Roy:
Use ³/4 ounce each of sweet and dry vermouth.

Green Briar:
Substitute Cointreau for the bitters.

80a–h.

RUM COCKTAILS

General
Description:

The many varieties and types of rum are well-suited to countless cocktail permutations. Early American colonists found the soil along the eastern seaboard unsuitable for growing grain to provide distilled spirits, and the European strains of grapevines did not grow well either. Sugarcane thrived in the Caribbean, however, and in its fermented state was easily and cheaply distilled into rum, making it the prevalent drink of the colonies. Rum was mixed with hot water, molasses, cider, and almost anything else, and various forms of rum mixtures were drunk from breakfast until bedtime. Gin eventually replaced rum as the alcohol of the poor, and rum drinks subsequently gained status, particularly during Prohibition. The rum cocktail's true ascension took place in Havana, where rum reigned supreme, in the creations of bartenders like Constantino Ribailagua of La Floridita. Rum drinks, especially the **Daiquiri**, greeted post-Prohibition drinkers with a new and refreshing face.

Another mostly neglected impetus for the rum

cocktail is the Chinese restaurant. As second-story chop suey joints moved downstairs and expanded their menu to include Polynesian dishes, they also imported the now-standard array of "exotic island drinks," all based on rum. With the occasional addition of 151-proof rum, just be careful you don't poke your eye out on the umbrellas.

Still, rum is not for everyone. To some, it is a plebeian upstart. Bernard DeVoto, in *The Hour*, virulently dismissed rum with a flick of his barbed pen: "People without tastebuds can enjoy it now. . . . No believer could drink it straight or gentled at the fastidious and hopeful hour. No one should drink it with a corrosive added, which is the formula of the Daiquiri." The more common rum drinks are listed in their particular entries, but some other diversions Mr. DeVoto would disapprove of are presented here.

Purchase:
There is hardly a bar in the world that will not offer some sort of rum drink.

Areas and Time of Occurrence:

Neighborhood watering holes may have one bottle of rum for the ubiquitous Rum and Tonic or Rum and Coke (**Cuba Libre**), but the well-stocked bar offers a bounty of rums in varying proofs and unusual flavors. The colonists may have partaken of it in the morning hours, but it is safe to say that breakfast is not the proper time to dip into a bottle of rum—which leaves the rest of the day for that venture.

Season:

Frosty and fruity rum cocktails are a mainstay of steamy summer months, but there are enough recipes and variations to cancel out every day on the calendar many times over.

Flavor Affinities:

Rum cocktails may immediately call to mind spareribs, nachos, and tempura, but they also go well with baked clams, barbecued chicken wings, and fajitas.

Recipes:

A Day at the Beach:
1 ounce coconut rum
$^1/_2$ ounce amaretto
4 ounces fresh orange juice
$^1/_2$ ounce grenadine
Wedge of pineapple and a maraschino cherry

Shake the coconut rum, amaretto, and orange juice with ice; then strain over ice into a chilled highball glass. Float the grenadine on top, and garnish with a pineapple wedge and a maraschino cherry.

Bahama Mama:
$^1/_2$ ounce dark rum
$^1/_2$ ounce light rum
$^1/_2$ ounce 151-proof rum
$^1/_2$ ounce Kahlúa
1 ounce fresh lemon juice
3 ounces unsweetened pineapple juice
Wedge of pineapple and a maraschino cherry

Shake the three rums, Kahlúa, lemon juice, and pineapple juice with ice; then strain over ice into a chilled highball glass. Garnish with a pineapple wedge and a maraschino cherry.

Black Maria:
2 ounces coffee-flavored brandy
2 ounces light rum
4 ounces black coffee
1 teaspoon superfine sugar

Stir all ingredients over ice in a brandy snifter.

Blue Hawaii:
1 ounce light rum
1 ounce blue curaçao
2 ounces unsweetened pineapple juice
1 ounce cream of coconut
Slice of pineapple and a maraschino cherry

Place the rum, blue curaçao, pineapple juice, and cream of coconut in a blender with a cup of cracked ice. Blend for 15 seconds, or until frothy. Pour into the strangest glass you can find, and garnish with a pineapple slice and a maraschino cherry.

Bolero:
Sugar for rimming
1¹/₂ ounces light rum

³/₄ ounce apple brandy
³/₄ ounce sweet vermouth
Twist of lemon peel

Rim a chilled cocktail glass with sugar. Shake the rum, brandy, and vermouth with ice; then strain into the cocktail glass. Garnish with lemon peel.

Continental:
1¹/₂ ounces light rum
1 tablespoon fresh lime juice
1¹/₂ teaspoons green crème de menthe
¹/₂ teaspoon superfine sugar
Twist of lemon peel

Shake the rum, lime juice, crème de menthe, and sugar with ice; then strain over ice into a chilled cocktail glass. Garnish with lemon peel.

Flirting with the Sandpiper:
1¹/₂ ounces light rum
3 ounces fresh orange juice
Dash of bitters
1 teaspoon cherry brandy

Shake the rum, orange juice, and bitters with ice; then strain over ice into a chilled highball glass. Float the cherry brandy on top.

Havana Cocktail:
1 ounce light rum
1/2 ounce fresh lemon juice
2 ounces unsweetened pineapple juice
Twist of lemon peel

Shake the rum, lemon juice, and pineapple juice with ice; then strain over ice into a chilled cocktail glass. Garnish with lemon peel.

Lounge Lizard:
1 ounce dark rum
1/2 ounce amaretto
4 ounces cold cola
Slice each of lime and orange

Mix the rum, amaretto, and cola over ice in a chilled old-fashioned glass. Garnish with lime and orange slices.

Skylab:
(adapted from an original by Tony Nettleton)
1 ounce 151-proof rum
1 ounce blue curaçao
1/2 ounce apricot brandy
1 ounce fresh orange juice
1 ounce unsweetened pineapple juice
1 ounce fresh lemon juice
1 teaspoon superfine sugar or simple syrup
Orange slice and a maraschino cherry

Stir together the rum, curaçao, brandy, orange juice, pineapple juice, lemon juice, and sugar over ice in a hurricane glass or large glass. Garnish with an orange slice and a maraschino cherry.

81. **RUSTY NAIL**

General
Description:

The Rusty Nail is a basic blend of Scotch and the Scottish liqueur Drambuie. Another amazingly simple drink, the Rusty Nail rounds out the classic triumvirate with the **Manhattan** and the **Rob Roy**. Judging from the number of drinks made with Scotch, this spirit never ceases to inspire elaborate and dizzying recipes, but the Rusty Nail is evidence that less is truly more. *Drambuie* is a Gaelic word for "the drink that pleases," and the liqueur is distilled from Scotch whisky. It was first produced on the Isle of Skye in the Inner Hebrides, supposedly from a recipe handed down by the eighteenth-century pretender to the British throne Bonnie Prince Charlie. And nothing could be less Scottish, save the recipe.

The Rusty Nail is strictly an American invention that became fashionable in the 1950s with people who wanted their Scotch without the bite of a Rob Roy. The name seems to indicate a fierceness, but the honeyed characteristic of Drambuie imparts a mellow tone. It is said that the Rusty Nail was named by one of several Scottish bartenders who repaid the incivility of loud American customers by stirring this drink with a rusty nail. One look at this ruddy amber cocktail would indicate the actual, albeit mundane, source of its name.

Purchase:

Bartenders in Scottish pubs will shoot you a dirty glance for asking them to bastardize two venerable drinks. Order a Rusty Nail elsewhere, or make it at home.

Areas and Time of Occurrence:

The Rusty Nail is open as to where and when it can be sipped. Its distinct overtones of honey make it a classic apéritif before a multicourse dinner. Its softness also lends itself to a hearty brunch. The Rusty Nail should in no way be excluded from your next Hibernian gathering or bagpipe jam session.

Season:

Served on the rocks, a Rusty Nail can be appreciated in a comfortable backyard deck chair on a tranquil spring afternoon. Heated slightly, it is a tailor-made winter warmer.

Preparation:

The essence of a Rusty Nail is its reddish glow. To appreciate it fully, serve it in fine cut-crystal with the clearest ice made from bottled water. The Rusty Nail is not served with a garnish.

Flavor Affinities:

The Rusty Nail is a robust drink that demands substantial foodstuffs. Mussels in a spicy vinaigrette, *kofta* (savory meatballs), and strong cheeses such as Stilton are up to the task.

Recipe:

Rusty Nail:
2 ounces Scotch
1 ounce Drambuie

Pour the Scotch and Drambuie over ice in a heavy old-fashioned glass, and stir.

Variation:

Aberfoyle:
Substitute vodka for the Scotch.

82a–c.

RYE COCKTAILS

General Description:

Use rye in drinks as you would bourbon. Waxing rhapsodic on the contribution of American spirits to the world, Bernard DeVoto, in *The Hour*, declared: "We have improved man's lot and enriched civilization with rye, bourbon, and the Martini cocktail." The Doors had a hit single with the Brecht-Weill "Alabama Song": "If we don't find the next whiskey bar, I tell you we must die." We know the whiskey was rye, because the line was inspired by the historian Arnold Toynbee, who said, "If I don't get rye whiskey, I surely will die." George Washington turned one of his failing farms into a bustling rye whiskey business.

Straight or blended, in the nineteenth century rye

was the essential drink and building block of most cocktails, but most people have never tasted it, nor do they even know what it really is, often mistaking Canadian Club for rye. Scotch began replacing rye in the 1930s, and after the repeal of Prohibition, rye all but vanished. Until fairly recently, only a few distilleries still produced it, but this is changing—and the true **Manhattan** may be restored to its proper place in the pantheon of cocktails. The more familiar rye drinks are listed in their particular entries, but a few old chestnuts worthy of revival are presented here.

Purchase:

With about eight brands of rye now available on the market, bartenders will soon be inventing new cocktails with this old spirit. But why not beat them to it and try it at home?

Areas and Time
of Occurrence:

Think of rye when you want to prepare a recipe with bourbon, and then see if it works. Rye cocktails have as much of a place in the upscale lounges and discothèques as any cocktail. Serve rye cocktails at your next party, and you will be instantly esteemed as being in the vanguard.

Season:

Straight up or on the rocks, sample a rye cocktail when in the mood for a whiskey-based drink.

Flavor
Affinities:

The versatility of rye sets the stage for a diversity of flavors. Onion tarts, beer-battered shrimp, and cheese and bacon bread rounds all complement the subtle sweet edge of rye.

Recipes: *Approve:*
2 ounces rye
2 dashes of Cointreau or triple sec
2 dashes of bitters
Twist each of lemon and orange peel

Shake the rye, Cointreau, and bitters with ice; then strain over ice into a chilled cocktail glass. Garnish with lemon and orange peel.

Opening:
2 ounces rye
1 ounce sweet vermouth
1 ounce grenadine
Maraschino cherry

Shake the rye, vermouth, and grenadine with ice; then strain over ice into a chilled cocktail glass. Garnish with a maraschino cherry.

Old Nick:
2 ounces rye
1 ounce Drambuie
¹/₂ ounce fresh orange juice
¹/₂ ounce fresh lemon juice

Dash of bitters
Twist of lemon peel

Shake the rye, Drambuie, orange juice, lemon juice, and bitters with ice; then strain over ice into a chilled cocktail glass. Garnish with lemon peel.

Rye Lane:
1¹/₂ ounces rye
1¹/₂ ounces fresh orange juice
2 dashes of almond-flavored liqueur

Shake the rye, orange juice, and liqueur with ice; then strain over ice into a chilled cocktail glass.

83. **SANGRÍA**

General
Description:

Sangría is a type of red punch made from red wine and fresh fruit, with an occasional addition of brandy. Nearly every restaurant in Spain serves sangría, and each has its own particular recipe. *Sangría*, which means "bleeding" in Spanish, was so named for its bold red color. The red wine–based drink attained a trendy notoriety in 1964 when it was introduced at the Spanish Pavilion at the New York World's Fair; it soon became a popular, refreshing party drink around the world. It briefly fell out of favor in the 1980s but has had a resurgence in the last decade. Sangría can also be made with white wine, but somehow Sangría Blanco—"white blood"—sounds curiously anemic. The Argentine sobriquet Clerico seems more fitting, however, and is used below for the white wine recipe.

Purchase:

Since every restaurant and bar makes sangría differently, the adventurous cocktailian will have to do a great deal of legwork and elbow work to find the best.

Areas and Time of Occurrence:

Because of the drink's numerous ingredients, bars remain the preferred spots to order sangría. However, mixing up several batches of sangría can be a money saver when hosting large parties. If especially pressed for time, you can prepare sangría in the morning and leave it until later. Pour the ruby beverage into a large punch bowl over a block of ice for an eye-catching centerpiece at a wedding or graduation, or bring out a pitcher for friends over a game of Scrabble and watch the words you begin to come up with.

Season:

Sangría is a refreshing drink all year, but switch to an icy Clerico to quell the heat of summer.

Preparation:

When making sangría at home, use a good-quality, assertive red wine. A Rioja or other Spanish wine will afford an authentic Spanish flavor, but a decent burgundy or Cabernet Sauvignon will also work. Chill the wine overnight. Always use fresh fruit, not a mix. Experiment with different fruits—kiwi, passion fruit, or even blood oranges. Be warned that eating too much of the alcohol-soaked fruit may have you seeing *elefantes rosados*—pink elephants.

Flavor
Affinities:

This is a Spanish punch, so tapas or other Spanish dishes work well here. Seafood lovers can feast on fried calamari or shrimp. Spicy meatballs, marinated mushrooms, and sharp cheese are full-bodied accompaniments to this fruity libation.

Recipes:

Sangría:
(Serves 4)
1 (750 ml) bottle Rioja or other red wine
2 teaspoons superfine sugar
1 lemon, sliced
1 orange, sliced
2 ounces Cointreau or triple sec
2 ounces brandy
12 ounces cold club soda

Pour the wine and sugar into a pitcher, and stir until the sugar is dissolved. Add the remaining ingredients, stir, and chill for an hour. Serve in chilled wine glasses.

Simple Sangría:
(Serves 4)
1 (750 ml) bottle Rioja or other red wine
2 ounces fresh lime juice
4 ounces brandy or light rum

12 ounces cold club soda
Assorted fruit as desired

Put all ingredients into a pitcher, and stir. Chill for an hour before serving.

Clerico (Sangría Blanco):
(Serves 4)
1 (750 ml) bottle dry white wine
2 teaspoons superfine sugar
1 banana, peeled and cut into chunks
1 orange, sliced
2 peaches, peeled and cut into 6 wedges each
1 red apple, peeled, cored, and diced
Juice of 1 lemon
½ cup seedless red grapes
12 ounces club soda or lemon-lime soda

Pour the wine and sugar into a pitcher, and stir until the sugar is dissolved. Add the remaining ingredients, stir, and chill for an hour. Serve in chilled wine glasses.

84. **SAZERAC**

General
Description:
⚠

The Sazerac is a cocktail originally made with rye; its unique flavor comes from the addition of Peychaud's Bitters and the Herbsaint. "She has a weakness for Sazerac Slings; give her even the fruit and she swings."

So go the lyrics to Stephen Sondheim's "Have I Got a Girl for You," from his 1970 Broadway hit *Company*. The Sazerac was en vogue during that era of experimentation with exotic cocktails, but now it is rarely found outside the city of its birth, New Orleans.

Creole apothecary Antoine Peychaud, who moved to New Orleans from the West Indies and set up shop in the French Quarter in the early 1800s, is credited with the earliest version of this drink. He mixed aromatic bitters from an old family recipe with brandy, water, and sugar for his ailing clients. What precisely ailed them is not known, but enough people suffered from the affliction that the concoction became the basis for what some historians claim to be the first true cocktail. While this is open to dispute, few will argue that the Sazerac is New Orleans's preeminent contribution to mixology. By the 1850s, the drink was served at the Sazerac Coffee House, which took its name from the Sazerac-de-Forget et Fils brandy imported by the establishment's owner, John B. Schiller. The bar changed hands, and new owner Thomas Handy updated the recipe by substituting American whiskey and adding a splash of absinthe for color—if not color-blindness. When absinthe was banned, Herbsaint, a New Orleans version of the licorice-tasting pastis, was introduced in its stead.

Both Peychaud's Bitters and Herbsaint are extremely difficult to come by outside Louisiana, sadly putting the cocktail on the endangered species list for the rest of the world. You can substitute ingredients, but that would be like exchanging a pair of high heels for fluffy bedroom slippers.

Purchase:

New Orleans is still the home of the Sazerac. Some specialty liquor shops carry Peychaud's Bitters and Herbsaint, but you can also mail order these ingredients to make this drink at home.

Areas and Time of Occurrence:

The Sazerac bar moved to the Roosevelt Hotel, which is now the Fairmont; here you can still order a Sazerac made according to the original recipe. Other New Orleans bars and restaurants, such as Commander's Palace and Galatoire, have developed their own versions of the Sazerac—much to the chagrin of each of the others. Until you can get to New Orleans, by all means shake up your own version of a Sazerac for your worthy friends.

Season:

In New Orleans, the **Hurricane** is considered a Mardi Gras cocktail washed down by the city's tourists, while the Sazerac is the locals' drink of preference throughout the year.

Preparation:

Sazerac aficionado Chuck Taggart admonishes those who substitute bourbon for rye. He cites legendary New Orleans bartender Stanley Clisby Arthur, who used to mix Sazeracs, as his defense. In *Famous New Orleans Drinks and How to Mix 'Em*, Arthur insists:

"While Bourbon may do for a julep it just won't do for a real Sazerac." If by chance you run out of rye—because there is no excuse not to have it except penury—substitute bourbon, but cognac or brandy is preferable to emulate the original recipe.

Flavor
Affinities:

Chilaquiles (spicy eggs on corn tortillas), gumbo, and fried oyster or shrimp rémoulade are favorite New Orleans dishes that may be served alongside a Sazerac.

Recipe:

Sazerac:
1 sugar cube
1¹/₂ ounces rye or American whiskey
2 dashes of Peychaud's Bitters
Dash of Angostura bitters
Dash of Herbsaint, Pernod, or Ricard
Twist of lemon peel

Fill an old-fashioned glass with ice. Put the sugar cube in a second old-fashioned glass with just enough water to moisten it; then crush the cube. Add the rye, the two bitters, and a few cubes of ice, and stir. Discard the ice from the first glass, and pour in the Herbsaint. Turn the glass to coat the sides with the Herbsaint; then pour out the excess. Strain the rye mixture into the herbsaint-coated glass. Twist and squeeze a lemon peel over the glass. Rub the rim of the glass with the peel, discarding it when finished.

85a–d.

SCOTCH WHISKY AND IRISH WHISKEY COCKTAILS

General
Description:

Scotch whisky and Irish whiskey are the foundations for innumerable cocktails. Blended Scotch and Irish whiskey have established themselves in numerous prominent cocktails, but they are less favored by bartenders for mixing cocktails than are American whiskies. Single-malt Scotch is much more smoky, and dyed-in-the-tartan single-malt drinkers have little time or patience with any divergence from tradition. Asked if they would like ice with their potent potable, they may irritably grumble that they are not in the mood for a mixed drink. Gary Regan, however, has flown in the face of tradition and blended single-malt cocktails. The more familiar Scotch whisky and Irish whiskey drinks are listed in their particular entries, but other noteworthy cocktails are presented here.

Purchase:

Although Scotch whisky and Irish whiskey are not as popular as other spirits for mixing, you will find them in abundance in most bars.

Areas and Time
of Occurrence:

People love Scotch, but sometimes you only hurt the one you love. Many modern lounges are mixing Scotch simply for the purpose of inventing new cocktails. This may be fine with most spirits, but rum and vodka are far more forgiving than whiskey. A well-made cocktail, however, is versatile enough to revive

the weary after a draining day at the office, perk up
your appetite for a great meal, and tuck you into bed
at night.

Season:

From invigorating cocktails served over craggy chunks
of ice in hefty rocks glasses to soothing **Hot Toddies**
sipped while watching the lightly falling snow, Scotch
whisky and Irish whiskey can work marvels on the
soul throughout the four seasons.

Flavor
Affinities:

Although hearty cheeses such as Stilton or double
Gloucester typically warrant port and walnuts, Scotch
cocktails have sweet undertones that would not be
amiss for this pairing. Try steak and kidney pie or fish
and chips for more substantial fare.

Recipes:

Affinity:
2 ounces Scotch
1 ounce sweet vermouth
2 dashes of bitters
Orange peel

Shake the Scotch, vermouth, and bitters with ice;
then strain over ice into a chilled cocktail glass. Flame
the orange peel (page 21), and use it as a garnish.

Bobby Burns:
1¹/₂ ounces Scotch
1¹/₂ ounces sweet vermouth

1 teaspoon Bénédictine
Twist of lemon peel

Shake the Scotch, vermouth, and Bénédictine with ice; then strain over ice into a chilled cocktail glass. Garnish with lemon peel.

Debonair:
(adapted from a recipe by Gary Regan)
2¹/₂ ounces Oban or Western Highlands
   single-malt Scotch
1 ounce Canton ginger liqueur
Twist of lemon peel

Stir or shake the Scotch and ginger liqueur with ice; then strain over ice into a chilled cocktail glass. Garnish with lemon peel.

Hoot Mon:
2 ounces Scotch
1 ounce sweet vermouth
1 ounce Lillet
Twist of lemon peel

Shake the Scotch, vermouth, and Lillet with ice; then strain over ice into a chilled cocktail glass. Garnish with lemon peel.

Loch Lomond:
2 ounces Scotch
¹/₂ ounce peach schnapps
1 ounce blue curaçao
3 ounces fresh ruby red grapefruit juice
1 teaspoon fresh lemon juice
Twist of lemon peel

Shake the Scotch, peach schnapps, blue curaçao, grapefruit juice, and lemon juice with ice; then strain over ice into a chilled hurricane glass. Garnish with lemon peel.

Scotch and Soda:

The English prefer just a splash of soda in this refreshing drink, and they will simply order it as a Whisky and Soda, the Scotch being a given.

To Hell with Swords and Garters:
(from a recipe cited by Gary Regan)
1¹/₂ ounces Scotch
1 ounce dry vermouth
1¹/₂ ounces unsweetened pineapple juice

Shake all ingredients with ice; then strain over ice into a chilled old-fashioned glass.

86a–c.

SCREWDRIVER

General
Description:

A drink with a lethal name—or a practical one, depending on your point of view—the Screwdriver is a basic mix of vodka and orange juice. The vodka version of the **Orange Blossom**, the Screwdriver has been around for a while. It was most likely the brainchild of master marketer John Martin, who popularized it to promote vodka after World War II. John Mariani, in his *Dictionary of American Food and Drink*, cites two sources for the drink's creation. According to one, oil-rig workers in the Middle East used screwdrivers to open cans of orange juice, which they then mixed with vodka to keep cool. The other source relates that a California bartender was experimenting with the new drinks at the request of an orange juice salesman. Upon asking one of his customers what he thought, the man is said to have replied, "I'd just as soon swallow a screwdriver." Let's face it, though, it's just orange juice and vodka, and it was probably just a nameless refresher before it became the Screwdriver. Give credit to Martin, though, for promoting it and transforming it into a classic cocktail. Along with the **Bloody Mary** and the **Moscow Mule**, the **Screwdriver** is in Martin's hat trick in the annals of marketing mixology. Of course, if you count the **Vodka Martini**—which he called the Vodkatini—Martin also hit for the cycle.

Purchase:	A staggeringly uncomplicated drink to make, the Screwdriver is universally available.

Areas and Time
of Occurrence:

One early Smirnoff ad campaign kicked off with the slogan "It leaves you breathless." Not only is plain vodka virtually tasteless, it also has no recognizable odor, which instantly makes it popular with anyone who wants to hoist back a nip or two without anyone noticing. The Screwdriver's simplicity and affability have made it a favorite drink to mix almost anywhere, anytime. A cold container of OJ and a pint of vodka conveniently transform laundromats, city parks, and the backseats of SUVs into portable bars. Screwdrivers are poured into paper cups on Friday afternoons at the office, beer mugs on Saturday nights in college dorms, and champagne glasses on Sunday mornings at brunch.

Season:

You always need vitamin C, which advocates for the Screwdriver as an all-season medicinal preventative.

Preparation:

If you do intend to mix a Screwdriver, mix it right. Never settle for ready-made orange juice when you can squeeze it fresh. It takes a little more time, but it makes a richer cocktail. And stay away from bargain-basement vodkas—they only lay the groundwork for a highway to Hangoverville.

Flavor
Affinities:

Substandard bar food or a big bag of ranch-flavored Doritos is the typical accompaniment, but this

sprightly cocktail also enhances prosciutto-wrapped
melon balls and sesame shrimp.

Recipe: ***Screwdriver:***
2 ounces vodka
5 ounces fresh orange juice
Slice of orange

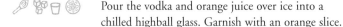 Pour the vodka and orange juice over ice into a
chilled highball glass. Garnish with an orange slice.

Variations: ***Cordless Screwdriver:***
Pour chilled vodka into a shot glass. Drink, and follow by biting into an orange wedge coated with
superfine sugar.

Melon Ball:
Substitute 1 ounce Midori melon liqueur for 1 ounce
of the vodka, and garnish with a small slice of honey-
dew melon.

Southern Screw:
Substitute 1 ounce Southern Comfort for 1 ounce of
the vodka, and garnish with a slice of orange.

Slow (Sloe) Comfortable Screw:
Substitute 1 ounce sloe gin for 1 ounce of the vodka.
Try asking your date if he or she would like this one.
Wait until at least the second date, though.

87a–c.

SEX ON THE BEACH

General
Description:

Sex on the Beach is one of many generic cocktails whose sole link is a reference to "doing it." What's in a name—indeed! Sex is often associated with cocktails, though such an observation would not surprise Freud or Kinsey, experts in the field. Sex on the Beach and its offspring are usually and appropriately called "shooters." Sex sells, and these drinks are particularly formulated with the libido in mind. Some of the wildly inventive names are meant to titillate, while others are blatant forays into potty talk. Winston Churchill or James Bond would never sidle up to the bar and request a Bald Pussy or a Tony's Screaming Weenie.

The names of these drinks are clearly fraught with double entendre—"I'd like a Screaming Orgasm, if you please." And as with real sex, these drinks come with their risks. The generally sweet but seriously potent concoctions go down so easily that multiple Orgasms will often lay the young toper out prone for the wrong reason. Not everyone wants Sex on the Beach. Joseph Scott and Donald Bain, in *The World's Best Bartender's Guide*, give the recipe for the variant Sleazy Sex on the Beach as follows: "Add 1 ounce of Grand Marnier, but only if you're feeling particularly wasteful and have little respect for Grand Marnier."

Purchase:

Sex on the Beach may be purchased wherever overactive libidos are rampant.

Areas and Time of Occurrence:	Singles bars were the original venues for Sex on the Beach, but to paraphrase the great Jimmy Durante, "Everybody wants to get into the unnatural act." Sex on the Beach and other tongue-in-cheeky-styled cocktails that were once endemic to pickup lounges are now popping up at food courts, bridal showers, and bar chains.

Season: "Mating season."

Flavor Affinities:	If music—and Sex on the Beach—be the food of love, then play on. That and a big bowl of party mix before, and anything in the fridge after.

Recipe: **Sex on the Beach:**
2 ounces vodka
2 ounces peach schnapps
3 ounces fresh orange juice or grapefruit juice
2 ounces cranberry juice

Stir all ingredients over ice in a highball glass.

Variations: **After Sex:**
Mix together 2 ounces vodka and 1 ounce crème de banane.

Orgasm:
Mix together 1 ounce amaretto, 1 ounce Kahlúa, and 1 ounce Bailey's Irish Cream.

Absolut Sex:

Mix together 1 ounce Absolut Kurant vodka, 1 ounce Midori melon liqueur, 1 ounce cranberry juice, and 1 ounce lemon-lime soda.

Screaming Orgasm:

Mix together 1 ounce vodka, 1 ounce Kahlúa, and 1 ounce Bailey's Irish Cream.

88a–b.

SHOOTERS AND SHOTS

General
Description:

Shooters and shots are mixed drinks meant to be served in a shot glass. "Barkeep, gimme a shot of whiskey, and leave the bottle." Those venerable words could belong to John Wayne or Humphrey Bogart—tough guys anesthetizing themselves into forgetfulness. The anesthetic effect is still there, but the main reason for knocking back shooters is flat-out inebriation in no time flat. The Brain Hemorrhage, the Surfer on Acid, the Mind Eraser, and other one-gulp wonders burst onto the bar scene in the 1970s and caused many a shaken head for bartenders and cocktail connoisseurs alike. The shooter has its origin in the **Pousse Café**, but unlike that meticulously layered cocktail, a shooter is a blend of sometimes unimaginable ingredients quickly shaken, poured into a shot glass, and downed in one greedy gulp. Shooters have become most fashionable, but the diehard classic cocktail drinker views this approach to alcohol the way one might view the Taliban's treatment of women.

Purchase:

Look for loud, rocking music and a touch of insanity, and a shooter will not be far behind.

Areas and Time of Occurrence:

☾

From the Long Island Iced Tea Shop in London to Shooters 52 in Hong Kong to N. N. Train Bar in Berlin to the Village Idiot in New York, shooters are everywhere. Like the shooter itself, lounges and bars featuring them are unabashed, unashamed, and out of control. Also note that just as Larry Talbot turned into the Wolfman under a full moon, a bar that serves shooters turns into a different animal at about 10 P.M. The shooter is definitely a drink for partying. Designated drivers wanted.

Season:

❄ ☀ ◇ ❄

Shooters are only served from January 1 to December 31.

Preparation:

Shooters may be served in fancy crystal shot glasses, but there is also a trend of serving them in the navel of a damsel stretched across the bar top. Make certain she has an "inny" if you want your money's worth. They may be served shaken or straight—the shooters, that is. Sometimes shooters are grasped by the teeth and drunk with hands behind the back. Do not attempt this with the navel. Bear in mind that the name's the thing here. You may order a Mind Eraser

252 *Field Guide to Cocktails*

#5 in five different places and get five different Mind Eraser #5s—but trying this is not recommended.

Flavor Affinities:

Forget Atkins if you do shooters—you will need the carbs to neutralize the booze. Cheese crisps, mini pizzas, chips and dip, and even a big bowl of sourdough pretzels are all recommended.

Recipes:

A Little Green Monster from Mars:
1 green maraschino cherry
¹/₂ ounce Jägermeister
¹/₂ ounce Rumple Minze

Remove the stem from the cherry, if present, and drop the cherry into a large shot glass. Pour in the Jägermeister and Rumple Minze, and serve.

Alabama Slammer (Slamma):
1 ounce Southern Comfort
1 ounce vodka
¹/₂ ounce sloe gin
¹/₂ ounce triple sec
¹/₂ ounce fresh lemon juice

Shake all ingredients with ice; then strain into a large shot glass.

Blow Job:
¹/₂ ounce Bailey's Irish Cream

¹/₂ **ounce orgeat**
Whipped cream

 Pour the Bailey's Irish Cream and orgeat into a shot
glass; then top with a dash of whipped cream.

Purple Hooter:
¹/₂ **ounce vodka**
¹/₂ **ounce Chambord**
Splash of 7-Up

 Shake all ingredients with ice; then strain into a large
shot glass.

Kamikaze:
1 part vodka
1 part triple sec
1 part Rose's Lime Juice

 Shake all ingredients with ice; then strain into a large
shot glass.

89a–c. **SIDECAR**

General
Description:

*A Sidecar is a methodical blend of brandy, Cointreau,
and fresh lemon juice.* When actor Robert Armstrong
is told by a policeman that the airplanes got King
Kong, he replies, "It wasn't the airplanes; it was beauty

killed the beast." Well, it was vodka that killed—or severely maimed—the Sidecar. By the 1930s, the brandy Sidecar was merrily rolling along. H. L. Mencken praised it as one of a dozen cocktails of any real worth. As vodka cocktails entered the fast lane, followed in tow by rum drinks, classics like the Sidecar were slowly left in the dust. One occasionally hears them being ordered in bars, but their resurgence is still wishful thinking.

The Sidecar has been with us at least since Prohibition, when the drink's authorship was claimed by Harry's New York Bar and named for a customer who arrived in the sidecar of a motorcycle. David Embury gives us his version in *The Fine Art of Mixing Drinks*: "It was invented by a friend of mine at a bar in Paris, during World War I, and was named after yet another motorcycle sidecar in which the good captain customarily was driven to and from the little bistro where the drink was born and christened." Based on these stories, one may ask why there are no Motorcycles, Taxis, or Velocipedes on bar menus.

Purchase: If you do find the Sidecar in your local lounge, chances are that your bartender uses a sour or lemon mix. Stick with straight lemon juice. Although an endangered species, the Sidecar is a classic obligatory for the home bartender.

Areas and Time of Occurrence: ☾	If there is a drink that can transport you back to another time, it is the Sidecar. When your **Daiquiri** seems to be wearing thin, resuscitate the Sidecar. When serving the Sidecar at home, create a mood by playing an old LP with "In the Mood" by Glenn Miller or anything by Tommy Dorsey or Count Basie.
Season: ❅☀❄❆	You may serve a Sidecar as a year-round cocktail, but also try it over the rocks during late July and August.
Preparation:	The Sidecar has undergone dramatic variations, but a classic Sidecar is always made with a harmony of tastes and contrasts in mind. It should be the precise ratio of sharp, sweet, and tart—and always cold. Some bartenders lightly sugar the rim of the glass for a further subtlety. Once again, use straight lemon juice in a Sidecar. Since the brandy in a Sidecar is there for its punch, you do not need to use your best brandy or cognac.
Flavor Affinities:	As exacting as the Sidecar is in its balance of flavors, its multiplicity is open to many different foods. Mini smoked sausage with mustard, Parmesan toasts, lobster bites, or the old mainstay bacon-wrapped chicken livers are but a few examples of the possible panoply of enticing offerings.
Recipes:	***Sidecar:*** **1 ounce brandy**

³/₄ ounce Cointreau
³/₄ ounce fresh lemon juice

 Pour all ingredients over ice into a chilled old-fashioned glass.

Variations:

Applecar:

Substitute applejack or apple brandy for the brandy.

Boston Sidecar:

Substitute ³/₄ ounce brandy and ³/₄ ounce light rum for the brandy, and fresh lime juice for the lemon juice.

Between the Sheets:
Sugar for rimming
³/₄ ounce brandy
³/₄ ounce light rum
³/₄ ounce Cointreau or triple sec
³/₄ ounce fresh lemon juice
Twist of lemon peel

 Rim a chilled cocktail glass with sugar. Shake the brandy, rum, Cointreau, and lemon juice with ice; then strain into the cocktail glass. Garnish with lemon peel.

BMW Sidecar:

Substitute Grand Marnier for the Cointreau.

90a–b. 📷 **SINGAPORE SLING**

General
Description:

In the early days, slings were generic drinks spiked with an alcoholic spirit and tempered by sweeteners and other ingredients. They evolved into beverages made with alcohol, water, and lime juice. A Gin Sling is ostensibly a **Gin Rickey**, which means that it is also a cooler, but the classic Singapore Sling warrants a category of its own. The Singapore Sling is a classic cocktail without a classic recipe; the recipe was lost during Prohibition. As for the precursors to the Singapore Sling, the original slings appeared at the end of the seventeenth century as a shot in the arm, and the belly, before breakfast. They were initially made with any "ardent spirits" mixed with sugar, mint, honey, and various herbs, but "sling" soon became a generic name for anything with a kick. Eventually, gin became the preferred ardent spirit, and bubbly soda water often replaced "still" water.

The Singapore Sling, also made with gin, first appeared at the Raffles Hotel in Singapore. Ngiam Tong Boon is credited with mixing the first Singapore Sling at the hotel's Long Bar somewhere between 1910 and 1915. Not content to leave history alone, another source identifies the port city of Sandakan in Borneo as the cocktail's place of origin; however, the Sandakan Sling has never made an appearance at the bar.

Purchase:	Every bartender you meet who makes a Singapore Sling naturally makes the most authentic and the best. You are judge and jury on this cocktail.
Areas and Time of Occurrence:	Arguments to its pedigree aside, when the Singapore Sling is done right, it has a complex marriage of flavors (as if marriage were not complex enough). The Long Bar still serves a version of the original that was "remembered" by one of its older bartenders. According to the Long Bar: "Originally, the Singapore Sling was meant as a woman's drink, hence the attractive pink color. Today, it is very definitely a drink enjoyed by all, without which any visit to Raffles Hotel is incomplete."
Season:	The convivial Singapore Sling is conducive, if not conductive, to all fair weather; summer or extremely warm weather is when this cocktail really shines.
Preparation:	Recipes and garnishes for slings can be simple or complex. The photographer in you can adorn a Singapore Sling with a ballsy lime peel or a festooned toothpick "flag" of pineapple and maraschino cherry. The only water to touch one version is ice, while others call for club soda. A splash of cold club soda is entirely optional.
Flavor Affinities:	Close your eyes and conjure up your favorite Chinese appetizers. Crunchy spring rolls, crab Rangoon,

spareribs, and pot stickers in a garlicky dipping sauce are all capital choices.

Recipes: ***Singapore Sling:***
(from the current Long Bar in Singapore)
3 ounces unsweetened pineapple juice
1¹/₂ ounces gin
¹/₄ ounce fresh lime juice
¹/₂ ounce Cherry Heering
¹/₄ ounce Bénédictine
¹/₄ ounce Cointreau
Dash of Angostura bitters
Wedge of pineapple and a maraschino cherry

Shake the pineapple juice, gin, lime juice, Cherry Heering, Bénédictine, Cointreau, and bitters with ice; then strain into a highball glass. Garnish with a pineapple wedge and a maraschino cherry on a toothpick.

Gin Sling:
2 ounces gin
¹/₂ ounce fresh lime juice
1 teaspoon grenadine
Cold club soda or water
Slice of orange

Pour the gin, lime juice, and grenadine over ice in a highball glass. Add club soda to fill; then garnish with slice of orange.

Variations: Vodka, Rum, Brandy, and Whiskey Slings may all be made by substituting the respective spirit for gin in the Gin Sling.

91.   **SOURS**

General
Description:
A sour is a not so much a drink as it is a concept. Lemon or lime juice, almost any liquor, and sugar—in proper proportion—form a sour. Don't even think about using a packaged mix for this cocktail. A simple but magical blend, the sour was first made with brandy in the middle of the nineteenth century. Bartenders have flirted with and still have their occasional flings with numerous other base alcohols, but whiskey was the liquor of choice by the end of the nineteenth century, with rye on equal footing with bourbon. Bourbon is still favored by many, but blended whiskeys and Scotch have jockeyed for position. Add a dash of grenadine to a Whiskey Sour, and you have the sophisticated **Ward Eight**.

Purchase: A perfect sour, be it Scotch, bourbon, or gin, is the test of a true bartender. The sour is also a fundamental drink for the home bartender.

Areas and Time
of Occurrence:
Sours have emerged from the drawing room and cocktail hour to become a perennial favorite anywhere from a summer smorgasbord to an early autumn

canning party. The sour is rarely drunk at brunches or as nightcap, but it is especially enjoyed from the late afternoon to the early evening. You will also find the Whiskey Sour at nearly every strip-mall pub chain, but you should not be looking there in the first place. Do not accept a sour from anyone offering it to you out of a creased brown-paper bag.

Season:

The tartness of lemon and the sweetness of sugar succeed in mellowing whatever season is upon you.

Preparation:

Always prepare sours fresh. Here is a foolproof rule of thumb for making a perfect sour every time: Mix 2 ounces of your chosen spirit with 1 teaspoon sugar and $3/4$ ounces lemon or lime juice (the "sour" flavor), and shake with cracked ice. Substitute lime juice for lemon in a Scotch Sour. Shake a sour well for a truly frothy drink, and serve it straight up in a cocktail glass, over the rocks in a hefty old-fashioned glass, or in a sour glass. Garnish with any assortment of seasonally fresh fruit.

Flavor Affinities:

Sours go with just about anything. Smoked salmon mousse, Indian lamb kebabs, or deep-fried cheese balls are among the many possibilities.

Recipe:

Whiskey Sour:
2 ounces rye or blended whiskey
$3/4$ ounce fresh lemon juice

1 teaspoon superfine sugar or simple syrup
Slice of orange or lemon (or both) and a
maraschino cherry

Shake the whiskey, lemon juice, and sugar vigorously with ice; then strain over ice into a chilled cocktail glass, old-fashioned glass, or highball glass. Garnish with an orange or lemon slice (or both) and a maraschino cherry.

Variations:

Vodka, Gin, Rum, Brandy, and Pisco Sours may all be made by substituting the respective spirit for the rye or blended whiskey in a Whiskey Sour.

92a–d.

STINGERS AND OTHER BEASTIES

General
Description:

Stingers, Grasshoppers, and Spiders are all generally built around white crème de menthe. Other insects may be derived from any combination of spirits intended to give you a buzz. The Stinger may need less clarification than **Punch**, **Flip**, or *sling*, but all these words clearly reflect the message in the bottle. The original Stingers were popular in New York at the end of the nineteenth century, when they were made exclusively with brandy. Cognac is as common as brandy in a Stinger nowadays. The Stinger developed a reputation as a sophisticate's drink, and it eventually attained an international appeal. The confirmed gin drinker

Somerset Maugham was said to set aside his usual for
an occasional Stinger, and Evelyn Waugh considered
it his cocktail of choice. As for the bite that gives you
a buzz, Scorpions and other like-named beasties are
listed below.

Purchase:

If you see the bartender reaching for a bottle of green
crème de menthe, order a different cocktail. He or she
has no clue how to make a real Stinger. This is another
classic that belongs in the home-bar repertoire.

Areas and Time
of Occurrence:

Stingers were initially postprandials or nightcaps, but
they have come to be appreciated before dinner as
well. Still, crème de menthe has a way of scaring off
even the most adventurous of revelers, and it is best to
serve Stingers at the end of a party, when your guests
are open to a little more experimentation.

Season:

As a nightcap, the Stinger is partial to no particular
season.

Preparation:

There is as much contention over whether to shake or
stir a Stinger as there is for any other drink. The glass
is also an issue, as is whether a Stinger should be
sweet or dry. Early recipes call for more crème de
menthe than do many contemporary versions. This is
because manufacturers have gradually made this
liqueur sweeter over the years. Green is simply not a
substitute for white.

Flavor Affinities:	The French customarily serve the cheese course after a meal, and a Stinger would pair very well with it. When diet-conscious guests forgo dessert, mix up a Stinger as an alternative.
Recipes:	**Stinger:** **2 ounces brandy or cognac** **1 ounce white crème de menthe**

Shake or stir the brandy and crème de menthe with ice; then strain over ice into a chilled cocktail glass, old-fashioned glass, or highball glass.

Variations: Vodka, Gin, Bourbon, and Rum Stingers may all be made by substituting the respective spirit for the brandy in a Stinger.

Grasshopper:
1 ounce green crème de menthe
1 ounce crème de cacao
1 ounce heavy cream

Shake all ingredients with ice; then strain into a chilled cocktail glass.

Scorpion:
1 ounce brandy
1 ounce light rum
3 ounces unsweetened pineapple juice

¹/₂ ounce orgeat
Dash of grenadine

Shake all ingredients with ice; then strain over ice into a chilled highball glass.

Scorpion Bowl:
(Serves 2)
6 ounces fresh orange juice
4 ounces fresh lemon juice
1¹/₂ ounces orgeat
6 ounces light rum
1 ounce brandy
Exotic flower

In a blender, mix the orange juice, lemon juice, orgeat, rum, and brandy with 2 cups crushed ice, and pour into a tiki bowl. Add ice cubes to fill. Garnish with an exotic flower.

Tarantula:
1¹/₂ ounces Scotch
¹/₂ ounce sweet vermouth
¹/₂ ounce Bénédictine
Twist of lemon peel

Shake the Scotch, vermouth, and Bénédictine with ice; then strain into a chilled cocktail glass. Garnish with lemon peel.

93. **SWIZZLES**

General
Description:

Swizzle names are based not on the alcohol used but on the method employed in preparing the drinks. Rum was the first alcohol used in this drink when it was first "swizzled" back in the 1800s. Whether the swizzle or the swizzle stick came first is another question. The drink hails from Jamaica, where a long, sturdy twig that fanned out at the bottom with tiny branches was used to mix it. Placing the twig between the palms of your hands, you rotated the ingredients and crushed ice rapidly in a glass, much the way a modern immersion blender works. Over time, the branch was replaced by a manufactured wood, glass, or metal paddle for the same purpose.

Although the practice of swizzling has been around for two centuries, John Mariani, in his *Dictionary of American Food and Drink*, dates the first mention of the term *swizzle stick* in print to 1879. As long as the drink is swizzled, it does not matter which spirits are used. The hundreds of swizzle sticks available today are simply long drink stirrers with palm trees, hula dancers, dolphins, and the usual list of suspect tiki designs attached at one end. It should also come as no surprise that the word *swizzled* also came to mean "drunk." The swizzle has been put on the endangered species list because most swizzle drinks are no longer truly swizzled, but are shaken or stirred.

Purchase: You probably won't find many bars that actually swizzle drinks, but try saying "swizzled, not stirred" and see what kind of reaction you get.

Areas and Time of Occurrence: Since only the most attentive and knowledgeable bartenders will know what real swizzles are, this cocktail is perfect for the home bartender who wants to impress friends at the next party.

Season: Swizzles are without a doubt among the most refreshing of summer drinks.

Preparation: Real swizzle sticks with fanned bottoms are available in specialty stores. Alternatively, metal fan whisks work just as well. Gyrate the whisk rapidly between your palms for an exceptionally frothy drink.

Flavor Affinities: Different swizzles will pair to flavors accordingly, and hot appetizers may go as well as cold. Ceviche, dips, and satay are universally appealing.

Recipe: ***Rum Swizzle:***
2 ounces rum
1 teaspoon superfine sugar or simple syrup
1 ounce fresh lime juice
Dash of Angostura bitters
Slice of lime

Pour the rum, sugar, lime juice, and bitters over crushed ice in a highball glass; then swizzle. Garnish with a slice of lime and a decorative swizzle stick.

Variations: **Vodka**, **Gin**, **Bourbon**, and **Rum Swizzles** may all be made by substituting the respective spirit for the rum in a Rum Swizzle.

94a–d.

TEQUILA COCKTAILS

General Description: *Tequila is distilled in a variety of styles with equally numerous flavor notes, making it ideal for a bounty of tequila cocktails.* For purists, there is only one way to drink tequila—take a slug of tequila, lick a spot of salt (traditionally mixed with powdered agave worm), and bite into a wedge of lime. Shaking of the head and wincing are not required. As tequila began creeping into bars, bartenders learned it was a serviceable replacement for rum, vodka, and gin; the first wave of tequila cocktails were virtual clones of slings, sours, and the **Martini**. Creative mixologists have concocted a second wave of tequila cocktails that surely stand on their own.

Purchase: Short of exclusive wine bars or temperance meetings, tequila cocktails are found everywhere.

Areas and Time of Occurrence: From bonfires on the beach to all-night jam sessions, from Tijuana Brass reunions to biker conventions, tequila cocktails are as common as piñatas at a birth-day party in Coatzacoalcos. Mexican restaurants are a given. People are always looking for new tequila cocktails with which to celebrate Cinco de Mayo. Think ahead and start planning on the previous September 16—the actual date of the Mexican Revolution.

Season: Some frosty tequila cocktails are more prevalent in the summer months, but tequila is refreshing year-round.

Flavor
Affinities: If your thoughts immediately run to Mexican food, follow them. Quesadillas, guacamole, spicy bean dips, and nachos with jalapeños all applaud cool tequila cocktails.

Recipes: **Brave Bull:**
2 ounces tequila
1 ounce Kahlúa
Wedge of lime

 Shake the tequila and Kahlúa with ice; then strain into a chilled old-fashioned glass with ice. Garnish with a lime wedge.

Hot Pants:
Wedge of lime and salt for rimming
2 ounces tequila
¹/₂ ounce peppermint schnapps
1 tablespoon fresh grapefruit juice

1 teaspoon superfine sugar or simple syrup
Wedge of lime

Rim an old-fashioned glass with lime and salt, and chill briefly. Shake the tequila, schnapps, grapefruit juice, and sugar with ice; then strain into a glass over ice. Garnish with a lime wedge.

Silk Stockings:
2 ounces tequila
1 ounce crème de cacao
1 ounce heavy cream
Dash of grenadine
Maraschino cherry and ground cinnamon

Shake the tequila, crème de cacao, cream, and grenadine with ice; then strain into a chilled sour or highball glass with ice. Garnish with a maraschino cherry and a dusting of cinnamon.

Tequila Mockingbird:
2 ounces tequila
3/4 ounce green or white crème de menthe
1 ounce fresh lime juice
Slice of lime

Shake the tequila, crème de menthe, and lime juice with ice; then strain into a chilled cocktail glass. Garnish with a lime slice.

95. 📷 **TEQUILA SUNRISE**

General
Description:

The primary use of grenadine is to color a drink, which is most evident in a Tequila Sunrise. The Tequila Sunrise is yet another drink in the long procession of cocktails born during the Prohibition era. Marion Gorman and Felipé de Alba, in *The Tequila Book*, suggest that the Tequila Sunrise was invented at the Agua Caliente racetrack for Californians who spent the night betting on the horses while drinking too much. The cocktail was considered to be a morning pick-me-up for the bettors—hence the name Tequila Sunrise. While absolutely plausible, the story may be just one more instance of the need to historicize a cocktail.

To tell whether a Tequila Sunrise is made right, watch the glass. Because of grenadine's specific gravity, it will begin to settle in the bottom of the glass beneath the glowing orange juice, a phenomenon that could have easily inspired its name. There is also a Tequila Sunset, which seems to have nothing to do with either theory of origin.

Purchase:

The Tequila Sunrise is a straightforward drink that all bartenders should know. It is also a primary drink that can be easily mastered at home.

Areas and Time
of Occurrence:

There is no need to order this drink at any racetrack after a night of carousing. Besides, by sunrise you should be in bed. The Tequila Sunrise over ice, however, does highlight brunch and is a nice departure from the usual Bloody Mary or Screwdriver. Straight up, it is a pleasant relaxant after a day of meetings or a final exam.

Season:

Mix up a Tequila Sunrise, and serve it whenever you would want a Screwdriver or other tart orange juice cocktail.

Preparation:

The trick to making a Tequila Sunrise work is all in the pouring. Think of it as a larger, and more salubrious, Pousse Café. Pour the ingredients slowly, and never over ice, or you will lose the effect. Therefore, chill the tequila first. If you decide to shake, omit the grenadine from the shaker and add it later. White tequila is always used.

Flavor
Affinities:

Mexican dishes such as warm black bean dip, crab tostadas, or chipotle meatballs are naturals here, but don't rule out Asian appetizers.

Recipe:

Tequila Sunrise:
1¹/₂ ounces white tequila, iced
4 ounces cold, fresh orange juice
Dash of grenadine
Slice of orange

Pour the tequila into a chilled highball glass, followed

by the orange juice. Float the grenadine on top, and garnish with an orange slice.

Variations:

Malibu Sunrise:
Substitute Malibu coconut rum for the tequila.

Sunrise on the Volga:
Substitute vodka for the tequila.

96. **TOM COLLINS**

General
Description:

The Tom Collins is a tall, cool drink that is not unlike a **Gin Fizz**. These two sour-based drinks, topped off with bubbly water, differ primarily in their distinct glasses and garnishes. Eyes wide shut, it is impossible to taste the difference between a Gin Fizz and a Tom Collins.

Those who have enjoyed a Tom Collins may not know it has a twin, the John Collins. They were born fraternal twins during the middle of the nineteenth century, but they have been cloned into identical twins for many bartenders today. As one might expect, a barkeep named Tom Collins is credited with creating the Tom Collins. Then where is John Collins? It is more likely that the "Tom" came from the sweet Old Tom Gin used in the drink, while "John" loosely referred to the more aromatic Dutch gin—*jenever*—mixed into a John Collins. Whatever the source, dry gin eventually became the spirit of preference for a Tom Collins, and whiskey replaced gin in a John Collins—for some. There are bartenders who see no distinction and make both with gin. Club soda, seltzer, and mineral water are readily available today, and Collinses have come to include vodka, rum, and even cognac. But sparkling waters were rather expensive, if not unobtainable, 150 years ago, and bicarbonate of soda was used then to give these cocktails their effervescence. Take two Alka-Seltzer in your Collins, and don't bother calling in the morning. If you still haven't had enough punishment and are a history buff, you can always try the Aqua Velva Collins. When soldiers during World War II ran dry, they would substitute this aftershave for gin.

Purchase: Differing schools of bartending will serve you their own Tom or John Collins. Ask if you are not sure, and try using that ceramic bottle of Dutch gin somebody gave you years ago for an authentic John Collins.

Areas and Time of Occurrence: Think of someone as relaxed as a tabby cat stretched out on a deck chair on a sultry afternoon and holding a tall, frosty glass beaded with droplets of condensation. Could there be a better time or place for a refreshing Tom Collins? The only thing warm about a Tom Collins is the friendship it tends to kindle.

Season:

With its full 14 ounces of cooling beverage over ice, the Collins is the paragon of summer satisfiers.

Preparation:

The Tom Collins was so much in demand in the nineteenth century that it had its own glass named for it. At 14 ounces, a collins glass holds 2 to 4 ounces more than the highball glass used for fizzes. Also unlike a fizz, the Collins always sports fruit, sometimes to the extreme. A cherry and an orange slice will do. Once again, ignore those bottles and packets of Collins mix, and build your drink from fresh fruit.

Flavor
Affinities:

Smoked salmon bites with fresh lemon or rolled prosciutto and provolone cheese rounds add a saltiness to the palate that makes these sparkling drinks even more welcome.

Recipe:

Tom Collins:
2 ounces gin
1 ounce fresh lemon juice
1 teaspoon superfine sugar or simple syrup
4 ounces cold club soda
Slice of orange and a maraschino cherry

Shake the gin, lemon juice, and sugar with ice; then pour into a chilled Collins glass filled with ice. Add the soda, and garnish with an orange slice and a maraschino cherry.

Variations:

John Collins:
Substitute whiskey or bourbon for the gin.

Vodka, **Brandy**, and **Rum Collinses** may all be made by substituting the respective spirit for the gin in a Tom Collins.

97a–f.

VODKA COCKTAILS

General
Description:

Good, straight vodka, being mostly tasteless and mostly potent, is the universal base for an endless array of vodka cocktails. Flavored vodkas have also become the base for innumerable recipes. Heublein president John Martin, also acknowledged for his contribution to the history of cocktails, promoted his signature drinks with a series of ad campaigns in the 1960s touting the purity of the product. Vodka's meteoric rise generated hundreds of competitors and has even led to a profusion of vodka bars. If you want to experiment with vodka cocktails using the myriad brands on the present-day market, you will have a different brand to try nearly every day for an entire year. Add to that the plenitude of flavored vodkas now en vogue, and the possibilities are endless. The more common vodka drinks are listed in their particular entries, but a few old and new vodka recipes are presented here.

Purchase:

Since vodka is everywhere, it's not so much an issue

of where you can purchase vodka cocktails as what you should order where. Know your biker bar, and don't ask for anything with a cherry unless the biggest dude in the place orders one first.

Areas and Time of Occurrence:

Vodka's sheer invisibility permits it to go where no other alcohol would dare—at least while anyone else is looking. Not only is vodka a furtive spirit, but it is also a drink you can have when you don't want to drink. Grapefruit juice, a little salt, and a nip of vodka gives us the benign Salty Dog, a welcome energizer after a late-night shift, when everyone else is just waking up. Vodka and apple juice make a seven-year-old's birthday party at the local pizzeria just that much more bearable. And don't the paintings at the community art exhibit look much finer when vodka is surreptitiously added to the 7-Up? This "86-proof nothing," as William Grimes called it, goes a very long way.

Season:

The versatility and adaptability of this potable make it open season all year long for the vodka cocktail.

Flavor Affinities:

The Russians customarily enjoy savory foods while imbibing their vodka: smoked salmon, dried sausages, and caviar when the purse permits.

Recipes:

Blue Lagoon:
1 ounce vodka

1 ounce blue curaçao
4 ounces lemonade

 Pour all ingredients over ice in a chilled highball glass, and stir.

Desert Sunrise:
1 ounce vodka
1¹/₂ ounces fresh orange juice
1¹/₂ ounces unsweetened pineapple juice
Dash of grenadine

 Shake all ingredients with ice; then strain into a chilled cocktail glass.

Salty Dog/Greyhound:
Pineapple juice and salt for rimming
2 ounces vodka
4 ounces fresh grapefruit juice

 Moisten the rim of a highball glass with pineapple juice, rim with salt, and chill. Pour the vodka and grapefruit juice over ice in the glass, and stir. Omit the salt for a Greyhound.

Dusty Dog:
2 ounces vodka
¹/₂ ounce crème de cassis
1 teaspoon fresh lemon juice

Dash of bitters
5 ounces ginger ale
Twist of lemon peel

Shake the vodka, crème de cassis, lemon juice, and bitters with ice; then strain into a chilled highball glass. Add the ginger ale, and garnish with lemon peel.

Road Runner:
2 ounces vodka
1 ounce amaretto
1 ounce coconut milk

Shake all ingredients with ice; then strain into a chilled cocktail glass.

Hazy Days of Winter (Vodka and Lime):
2 ounces vodka
Cold bottled water
Twist of lime peel

Pour the vodka and water to fill over ice in a chilled old-fashioned glass, and stir. Garnish with lime peel.

Volga Boatman:
2 ounces vodka
1 ounce kirsch
1 ounce fresh orange juice
Maraschino cherry

Shake the vodka, kirsch, and orange juice with ice; then strain into a chilled cocktail glass. Garnish with a maraschino cherry.

98a–d. **VODKA MARTINI (STALINI) AND OTHER "TINIS"**

General
Description:

*The Vodka Martini, Stalini, or Vodkatini is the vodka-based version of the **Martini**.* Since the birth of the Vodka Martini, it seems another "tini" has been born practically every minute. As noted in its own entry, the original Martini passed through its colorful history with changes, refinements, embellishments, and several claimants to its authorship. In the case of vodka, its Martini history is glossed over, primarily because there is none. Sometime during the late 1950s, as vodka itself climbed in sales, people began ordering vodka instead of gin. In Tennessee Williams's 1959 play *Sweet Bird of Youth*, the character Chance orders a Martini and receives a classic gin variety with olives. He complains, "Everybody drinks vodka martinis with lemon twist nowadays."

The lineage of the classic Martini is prodigious, and while the Vodka Martini's history is slight by comparison, the cocktail has fended off the slings and arrows of Martini purists to become a formidable opponent. Despite sharing the same name, physical appearance, and basic alcohol content, the two might as well be polar opposites for their respective adherents. Most Vodka Martini drinkers loathe the harsh taste of gin, and Gin Martini drinkers often dismiss the Johnny-come-lately as a tasteless upstart. William Grimes, in *Straight Up or On the Rocks*, bemoans the rise of the Vodka Martini: "The logic of the martini has turned the drink inside out. It now glows in perfect transparency—sans vermouth, sans botanicals, sans everything."

But the Vodka Martini is not going anywhere but up. Credit for its success must be given in part to John Martin, the tireless promoter of his own brand Smirnoff and of the Vodkatini, but the Vodka Martini owes its legitimization as a sophisticated cocktail to Ian Fleming's urbane secret agent, James Bond. Since more brands of vodka began appearing worldwide, culminating in the 1990s watershed of designer vodka, the Vodka Martini has become a classic in its own right, outselling its progenitor three to one. Many of those who concede that the Vodka Martini merits its rank and praise also believe that it deserves its own name. After all, **Manhattans** and **Rob Roys** have theirs. Michael and Jane Stern's Roadfood Web site hosted a contest among its thousands of "Roadfooders" to come up with the Vodka Martini's own moniker. "Stalini" was chosen, and Roadfooders have attempted to bring the name into the mainstream as a substitute for "Vodka Martini." The Stalini is just one example of how present-day Vodka

Martini fanatics are helping to create a mythos that the cocktail sorely lacked.

Divergent as the Martini and Vodka Martini may be, the mystique, allure, and sophistication of these drinks have made them permanent fixtures in the world of cocktails. Regarding proportions, preparation, and garnishes for "Vodka Martini," if there is one thing all Martini drinkers agree on, it is nothing.

Purchase: See **Martini**.

Areas and Time of Occurrence: See **Martini**.

Season: See **Martini**.

Preparation: See **Martini**.

Flavor Affinities: See **Martini**.

Recipes: ***Vodka Martini (Stalini):***
3 ounces vodka
Dry vermouth
Green olives or twist of lemon peel

Depending on your taste, mix 5 to 8 parts vodka to 1 part vermouth for a dry Martini, but diminish the vermouth to taste for a drier Martini. Stir in a pitcher half filled with ice, or shake with ice; then strain into a chilled cocktail glass. Garnish with green olives or lemon peel.

Variations:

French Martini:

Substitute Chambord for the vermouth, and add 1 ounce pineapple juice.

Rumtini:

Substitute light rum for the vodka, and garnish with a twist of lime peel.

Tequini:
Substitute tequila for the vodka, and garnish with a twist of lime peel.

Apple Martini:
2 ounces vodka
1 ounce apple schnapps
1 ounce apple juice (optional)
Slice of apple

Shake the vodka, apple schnapps, and apple juice with ice; then strain into a chilled cocktail glass. Garnish with an apple slice.

Sour Apple Martini:

Substitute Sour Apple Pucker in the Apple Martini recipe, and garnish with a slice of Granny Smith apple.

Chocolate Martini:
Unsweetened cocoa powder, for rimming
1 ounce dark crème de cacao, plus more for
rimming
2 ounces vodka
Dark or milk chocolate truffle

Moisten the rim of a cocktail glass with crème de cacao, rim with cocoa powder, and chill the glass. Shake the crème de cacao and vodka with ice; then strain into the glass. Garnish with a dark or milk chocolate truffle.

White Chocolate Martini:

Using the Chocolate Martini recipe above, omit the cocoa, and substitute white crème de cacao for the dark crème de cacao.

---

99. **WARD EIGHT**

General
Description:

The Ward Eight is a unique variation on a sour. Some classic cocktails, like the **Bronx**, have become dinosaurs, and others, like the **Martini**, have engendered incalculable variations. The Ward Eight is one old-timer that has not been ravaged by time. While the name may have one conjecturing a drink so potent that it was named for a mental ward, the history of the Ward Eight is colorful but rather sober and sedate.

In 1898, bartender Tom Hussion was hired by the Locke-Ober Café in Boston, and he brought with him many loyal followers. Among them were members of the Hendrick's Club, a political club run by Democrat Martin Lomasney. Lomasney was running for representative in the Massachusetts General Court from Ward Eight that year, and the eve before the election, some club members at the bar asked Hussion to create a new drink to toast Lomasney's imminent victory. Hussion may have merely added some grenadine to a Whiskey Sour and called it the Ward Eight, but the grenadine was just enough to change the character of the drink. Ironically, the newly elected Lomasney was a staunch Prohibitionist, and when the Noble Experiment arrived, the owner of the Locke-Ober sorrowfully closed the bar. The Ward Eight outlasted Prohibition and was deemed one of the ten best cocktails of the year in 1934 by *Esquire* magazine. The Locke-Ober reopened its doors in the early 1950s and has been shaking up this sophisticated cocktail ever since.

Purchase:

The Ward Eight is another reason to visit Beantown, but this classic cocktail should also be in the arsenal of every straight-shooting home bartender.

Areas and Time of Occurrence:

☾

The Locke-Ober restaurant and bar is the paradigm of the unhurried elegance of the late nineteenth century—according to the Locke-Ober PR team. But they are right. Ordering a Ward Eight in the opulent surroundings is like traveling back in time. Serve this drink at your most formal cocktail or dinner parties.

Season:

❄ ☀ ❄ ❄

Order a Ward Eight just as you would order a Martini, a **Manhattan**, or any other classic cocktail. Election Day is the perfect day to prepare it at home, since bars in many states are closed that day.

Preparation:

A Ward Eight is always shaken. The cocktail may be garnished with a cherry or an orange or lemon slice for color, but these were omitted in the original. Rye was initially used, but bourbon seems to have taken its place as the liquor of choice.

Flavor Affinities:

Boston is noted for its fresh seafood, and crab cakes, clams, and oysters should be your first pick. Steak tartare, composed of minced raw sirloin, chopped onions, capers, and anchovies bound together with an egg yolk, fresh lemon juice, and a splash each of Worcestershire and Tabasco sauce, is still a Locke-Ober classic.

Recipe:

Ward Eight:
2 ounces rye or bourbon
¹/₂ ounce fresh lemon juice
¹/₂ ounce fresh orange juice
1 teaspoon grenadine
Maraschino cherry (optional)

Shake the rye, lemon juice, orange juice, and grenadine with ice; then strain over ice into a chilled cocktail glass. Garnish with a maraschino cherry, if desired.

100. **WATER DRINKS**

General Description:

Taken for granted, water in its natural state is vital for many cocktails. Most people would agree that when it comes right down to it, water is the most satisfying of potables. Fortunately, it never comes right down to it. Without delving into the history of water—it has been around for a long time—as a potable, water has been both cherished and disparaged throughout time. In fact, until the twentieth century, when water became subject to purification and stricter pollution standards, water has had a rather murky history, and many people rarely drank it straight unless forced to. Explorers and émigrés were accustomed to the contaminated water of Europe, and when the colonists settled in America they took to drinking or mixing water only gradually. Bourbon and branch water harkens back to the nineteenth century in America, when water was still suspect. But don't look for branch water in stores, as it was merely water from a fresh running stream, a "branch." Water went on to become a necessary mixer and chaser for the gritty booze of the Prohibition era.

Contemporary tastes may prefer the crisp fizziness of carbonated water in drinks, but don't discount still water. Excluding single-malt Scotch, almost all whiskey benefits from the addition of a little water, which opens up the whiskey in most cases. The water used to dilute the strength of your drink should be still and not too high in minerals. Water is also imperative for most **Hot Toddies**, **Punches**, the **Mint Julep**, the **Blue Blazer**, and the much-maligned **Jell-O Shot**. At the risk of being screamingly obvious, some elementary water drinks are presented here for the sake of thoroughness.

Purchase:

Purchase water drinks from bars that treat all their spirits with equanimity. Just as poor ice can damage a drink, so can bad water. If you have metallic or "funny" tasting water at home, use only bottled water—and for your ice as well.

Areas and Time of Occurrence:

One might guess that the obvious place to find water drinks would be in local watering holes. Scotch and Water and other water drinks are welcome potables after work to help you unwind. They are also mild relaxants at the end of the evening when you want just a little something more but don't want to indulge in anything that will make you sorry in the morning.

Season:

Like water itself, water drinks know no season.

Preparation: If you are unsure of the source, taste your water first. It's always best to add water to a drink a little at a time. As a rule of thumb for Scotch or bourbon, older whiskey needs less water. Whiskey aged in sherry casks loses its subtlety when too much water is added, and the aromas also break up. That said, Macallan has introduced a "cask strength" single malt—at 114.8 proof—that flies in the face of tradition and requests the addition of water or ice.

Flavor Affinities: Keeping in mind that the spirits you use will become more diluted as your ice melts, choose foods that will not overpower your drink. Mild cheeses or assorted cold cuts and crackers are homey accompaniments.

Recipes: ***Scotch and Water:***
2 ounces Scotch
4 ounces cold bottled water, or to taste

Pour both ingredients over ice in a chilled highball glass, and stir.

Bourbon and Branch Water:
2 ounces bourbon
4 ounces cold bottled water

Pour both ingredients over ice in a chilled highball glass, and stir.

101a–c.

WINE COCKTAILS

General
Description:

Wine cocktails may derive from any form of fermented grape. It is fitting that wine follows water, if only for alphabetical consistency. Wine has been with us nearly as long as water, but in all that time, no one has attempted to change wine into water. Although not often thought about, wine is the basis for many standard cocktails. Vermouth, Lillet, sherry, and champagne are all technically wine. Young strong wine, which is often heavy on its own, is an excellent partner for juices, soda, and fruit for long, cool drinks. In fact, the earliest wine was always mixed with water, and the ancient Greeks had specific vessels for water, wine, and mixing. Never use exceptional, vintage wines for cocktails, even if you are feeling extremely flush. Fine wines will suddenly forget who they are and diminish into the unrecognizable. Besides, younger wines will simply taste better. **Sangría** and **Champagne Cocktails** are found under their own headings.

Purchase:

Most exclusive wine bars will look at you askance if you order even as much as a spritzer of wine and club soda, and cocktail lounges will likely have "jug" wine. Order wine cocktails at a restaurant bar with a decent wine menu. Wine cocktails are particularly appealing for casual parties at home.

**Areas and Time
of Occurrence:**

Wine cocktails have less alcohol than most other cocktails, and they are therefore worth considering in restaurants as an alternative to beer. White wine is more commonly found in wine cocktails, making these cocktails better suited for outdoor gatherings in the afternoons or over leisurely barbecues. Short wine cocktails are interchangeable as apéritifs, and warmed wine makes for a friendly late-night **Hot Toddy**.

Season:

Season depends on the base of your wine cocktail, but rest assured that there is a wine cocktail for every season.

**Flavor
Affinities:**

The old adage "red wine with meat, and white wine with fish" may be applied here as a basic rule of thumb, but savory dishes also welcome reds, and lighter fare may be more suited to whites. As complex as wine can be, so can the choices. Cheese in its myriad forms always goes well, and most canapés and appetizers, as long as they are not acidic, will do nicely.

Recipes:

Broken Spur:
2 ounces port
²/₃ ounce sweet vermouth
¹/₂ teaspoon Cointreau or triple sec
Twist of lemon peel

Shake the port, sweet vermouth, and Cointreau with ice; then strain over ice into a chilled cocktail glass. Garnish with lemon peel.

Hillary Wallbanger:
4 ounces Chardonnay or other dry white wine
2 ounces fresh orange juice
¹/₂ ounce Galliano

Pour the Chardonnay and orange juice over ice in a chilled collins glass. Stir, and then float the Galliano on top.

White Wine Spritzer:
4 ounces Chardonnay or other dry white wine
2 ounces cold club soda
Twist of lemon peel

Pour the Chardonnay and club soda over ice in a chilled wine glass, and stir. Garnish with lemon peel.

Claret Lemonade:
1 teaspoon superfine sugar or simple syrup
2 ounces fresh lemon juice
2 ounces dry red wine
Cold water
Slice of lemon and a maraschino cherry

Add the sugar and lemon juice to a chilled highball glass, and muddle until the sugar dissolves. Add ice, the wine, and then cold water to fill. Garnish with a lemon slice and a maraschino cherry.

102. **ZOMBIE**

General
Description:

Every so often a simple relaxing drink comes along with an equally carefree name. The Zombie is not one. The name conjures up such bygone film stars as Karloff and Lugosi with good reason. The nine-odd ingredients in a Zombie make for a lethal brew that is more the product of a mad scientist than a bartender.

The first Zombie was created by Ernest Raymond Beaumont-Gant (who for some obscure reason was called "Don the Beachcomber") in the 1930s as a hangover cure for a patron at Don's Los Angeles bar. The fellow returned to the bar a few weeks later, and Don asked him how he liked the drink. The customer replied, "I felt like the living dead." The Zombie went on to become the signature drink at the Hurricane Bar at the 1939 World's Fair in New York, and Trader Vic featured it on his menu. It has since become a standard drink at Chinese restaurants, where it continues to transform jovial patrons into the moribund characters of a George Romero flick. The addition of 151-proof rum likens the Zombie to a postmortem in a glass.

Purchase:

Anywhere you spy a tiki statue, a paper drink parasol, or sticks of bamboo, you will find a Zombie lurking. Beware the dreaded premixed Zombie.

Areas and Time of Occurrence: 	You may want to think twice before you order one of the world's most lethal cocktails, because you may not be able to think at all afterward. If you do decide to seek out one of these weapons of mass destruction, Polynesian lounges like Trader Vic's and other high-end resort hotels mix their Zombies fresh. Otherwise, Zombies are usually prefab concoctions. Not counting the option of never, the time to order a Zombie is with appetizers before dinner.
Season:	The Zombie may strike you as a summertime drink, but it will strike you whatever the season.
Preparation:	The first Zombies were probably shaken, but the drink is more commonly mixed in a blender today. The daunting array of ingredients may persuade you to forgo fresh fruit juices, but if you are going to hell in a handbasket, the handle should be well made.
Flavor Affinities:	Since the Zombie is the equivalent of a liquid pupu platter, indulge yourself and order that tiny hibachi surrounded by barbecued beef sticks, crab Rangoon, chicken, prawns, and crisp wontons.
Recipe:	***Zombie:*** **³/₄ ounce fresh lime juice** **1 ounce unsweetened pineapple juice** **1 ounce fresh orange juice** **1 ounce light rum**

1 ounce dark rum
$^{1}/_{2}$ ounce apricot brandy
1 ounce passion fruit syrup
1 teaspoon superfine sugar
$^{1}/_{2}$ ounce 151-proof rum
Maraschino cherry, slice of orange, slice of pineapple, and a sprig of mint

Shaker method: Shake the three juices, light and dark rum, brandy, passion fruit syrup, and sugar with ice; then strain over ice into a chilled hurricane or other large glass. Float the 151-proof rum on top; then garnish with a maraschino cherry, an orange slice, a pineapple slice, and a mint sprig.

Blender method: Blend the three juices, light and dark rum, brandy, passion fruit syrup, and sugar with $^{1}/_{2}$ cup crushed ice. Pour into a hurricane glass, and float the 151-proof rum on top; then garnish with a maraschino cherry, an orange slice, a pineapple slice, and a mint sprig.

Drink Measurements and Calculators

Drink Measurements

1 dash	$1/32$ ounce (0.9 milliliter [mL])
1 teaspoon	$1/8$ ounce (3.7 mL)
1 tablespoon	$1/2$ ounce (14.8 mL)
1 pony	1 ounce (29.5 mL)
1 ounce	$1/8$ cup (29.5 mL)
1 jigger	$1^1/2$ ounces (44.5 mL)
$1/2$ cup	4 ounces (118 mL)
1 cup	8 ounces (237 mL)

Bottle sizes

750 milliliters	25.4 ounces
1 liter	33.8 ounces
1.75 liters	59.2 ounces

Drink Calculator per Bottle for Cocktails

750 milliliters	16 drinks
1 liter	22 drinks
1.75 liters	38 drinks

Drink Calculator per Number of People at a Cocktail Party

6 people	12–18 drinks
8 people	16–24 drinks
10 people	20–30 drinks
12 people	24–36 drinks
20 people	40–60 drinks
30 people	60–90 drinks

Density Chart

Since different brands of same-flavored liqueurs may have different sugar contents, which will affect the density, it may be necessary to practice before serving the Pousse Café to guests. If you like cream, add it at the end, as it will float on most liqueurs.

HEAVIEST

Grenadine
Crème de Cassis
Crème de Noyaux
Anisette
Crème de Almond
Kahlua
Crème de Banane
Dark Crème de Cacao
White Crème de Cacao
Coffee liqueur
Cherry liqueur
Green Crème de Menthe
White Crème de Menthe
Strawberry liqueur
Blue Curacao
Galliano
Blackberry liqueur
Amaretto
Triple sec
Tia Maria
Apricot liqueur
Drambuie
Frangelico

Curacao
Benedictine
Apricot brandy
Sambuca
Blackberry brandy
Cherry brandy
Peach brandy
Campari
Yellow Chartreuse
Midori melon liqueur
Rock and Rye
Cointreau
Peach schnapps
Sloe gin
Kummel
Peppermint schnapps
Benedictine
Brandy
Green Chartreuse
Water
Tuaca
Southern Comfort

LIGHTEST

Selected Bibliography

A number of splendid cocktail books are available, from books that cover single subjects (such as the Martini) to comprehensive drink recipe books. A serious collector should attempt to find Bernard DeVoto's *The Hour*. Lowell Edmunds enumerates early bartender's manuals on his Web site: www-rci.rutgers.edu/~edmunds/barman.html. William Grimes's *Straight Up or On the Rocks* is an exhaustive history of the American cocktail; Alec Waugh's *Wines and Spirits* is a noteworthy study of drink throughout the world. Bartender supreme Gary Regan has written an exceptional slim volume with his wife, Mardee, called *New Classic Cocktails*, and the maestro and alchemist of the cocktail, Dale DeGroff, has written the classic *The Craft of the Cocktail*.

Amis, Kingsley. *On Drink*. London: Jonathan Cape, 1972.

Arthur, Stanley Clisby. *Famous New Orleans Drinks and How to Mix 'Em*. Greta, LA: Pelican, 1989.

Barr, Andrew. *Drink: A Social History of America*. New York: Carol & Graf, 1999.

Conrad, Barnaby. *The Martini*. San Francisco: Chronicle Books, 1995.

Cipriani, Arrigo. *Harry's Bar*. New York: Arcade, 1996.

Craddock, Harry. *The Savoy Cocktail Book*. London: Constable and Company, 1930.

DeGroff, Dale. *The Craft of the Cocktail*. New York: Clarkson Potter, 2002.

DeVoto, Bernard. *The Hour*. Cambridge, MA: Riverside, 1951.

Edmunds, Lowell. *Martini, Straight Up*. Baltimore: Johns Hopkins University Press, 1998.

Embury, David. *The Fine Art of Mixing Drinks*. New York: Doubleday & Co., 1948.

Grimes, William. *Straight Up or On the Rocks*. New York: Simon & Schuster, 1993.

Herbst, Sharon Tyler, and Ron Herbst. *The Ultimate A-to-Z Bar Guide*. New York: Broadway, 1998.

Johnson, Harry. *New and Improved Bartender's Manual, or How to Mix Drinks of the Present Style*. N.p., 1888.

Mariani, John. *The Dictionary of American Food and Drink*. New York: Hearst Books, 1994.

Mario, Thomas. *Playboy's Host and Bar Book*. Chicago: Playboy Press, 1971.

Mr. Boston. *Official Bartender's and Party Guide*. New York: Warner Books, 2000.

Price, Pamela Vandyke. *Dictionary of Wine and Spirits*. London: Northwood Books, 1980.

Regan, Gary. *The Bartender's Bible*. New York: HarperPaperbacks, 2000.

Regan, Gary. *The Joy of Mixology*. New York: Clarkson Potter, 2003.

Regan, Gary, and Mardee Haidin Regan. *New Classic Cocktails*. New York: Macmillan, 1997.

Scott, Joseph, and Donald Bain. *The World's Best Bartender Guide*. New York: HPBooks, 1998.

Thomas, Jerry. *The Bar Tender's Guide, or How to Mix All Kinds of Plain and Fancy Drinks*. New York: Dick & Fitzgerald, 1887.

Waugh, Alec. *Wines and Spirits*. New York: Time-Life Books, 1968.

Index

Numbers in **bold** (for example, **18**) can be used to locate cocktails in the photograph section. All other numbers are page numbers.

More Quirk Field Guides

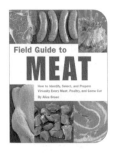

Field Guide to
MEAT

How to Identify, Select, and Prepare
Virtually Every Meat, Poultry, and Game Cut
By Aliza Green

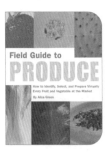

Field Guide to
PRODUCE

How to Identify, Select, and Prepare Virtually
Every Fruit and Vegetable at the Market
By Aliza Green

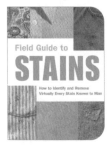

Field Guide to
STAINS

How to Identify and Remove
Virtually Every Stain Known to Man

Field Guide to
TOOLS

How to Identify and Use Virtually Every
Tool at the Hardware Store
By John Kelsey

Available Wherever Books Are Sold